ROCKIN THE VB.NET INTERVIEW

A comprehensive question and answer reference guide for the VB.Net programming language including MVC, ASP.Net, Entity Framework, WCF, Silverlight and object oriented programming.

Written by Greg Unger

Ordering Information

Quantity sales. Special discounts are available on quantity purchases by corporations, associations, and others. For details, contact us.

Orders by U.S. trade bookstores and wholesalers, please contact us.

Contact Information

Email address: businessathlete101@gmail.com

Website: http://www.thebestsellingbooks.org

Dedication

Dedicated to all the programmers who didn't get the job because they just didn't have the knowledge they needed. Those who have a hard time remembering reference materials off the top of your head, this book is for you.

Hopefully this levels the playing field and gets you the job of your dreams. You deserve it!

Table of Contents

Foreword

This book is broken up into sections by subject. You will find
redundancy in some of the questions because they cross-pertain
to multiple subjects. This makes it easier to skip to one subject or
another without any cross dependency. Some of the questions
are very simple and some are very difficult. I would suggest you
know the answers to all of these questions even if you just
memorize the answer I give. The answers are very short and to
the point. If you feel you are lacking understanding of either the
question or the answer, I urge you to do further reading. This is
your professional and like any profession you need to become a
master at what you do. You must know the language you are
programming in inside and out to be the best programmer you
can be.

Do not worry if you need to re-read this book a few times. Most
people will need to. I find it useful to have Visual Studio open
when reading a book like this so I can review in practice things I
learn while reading.

I tried to make this as comprehensive as possible without turning
this into a reference guide. By no means is this book exhaustive.
I could add another couple hundred pages to this and still not
cover everything that could be covered given the topics I have
included in this book.

You will find that I do not group the questions in sections very
often. I do this purposely to make it your brain have to work a
little bit harder in order to commit the information to memory.

CHAPTER 1: INTERVIEW BASICS

Your attitude

Let me start out with first things first. Your attitude is going to play possibly the biggest role in whether or not you will get a job. Because of this we need to get you prepped for what your state of mind should be before you sit down in front of the interviewer.

As with almost all aspects of life, everyone gets better with practice.

To be a top contender for a job, there is nothing better than a successful interview, yet interviews can be intimidating prospects. Here are some suggestions to help you prepare to present yourself at your best.

Assess your skills and experiences

• Focus on three to four areas where your skills are the strongest. Knowing these will help you tell your interviewer why they should hire you.

• Practice describing your special talents and skills.

• Examine your work and education background. Look for skills and experiences that match the job description.

Create a list of experiences to relate

Employers want real examples of how you behave professionally.

• Identify examples that relate to the job description and where you have performed well using your skills and background.

Practice relating the experiences aloud

• Organize your thoughts and communicate clearly.

- Explain the situation

- Describe your role or task

- The action you took

- The results of your action

• Include what you learned or what you might do differently in the future.

• Memorize your answers ahead of time but do NOT come off like the answers were memorized. No one wants to listen to a scripted, pre-recorded message but you also want to make sure you say the right thing.

Organizing your thoughts ahead of time and practicing them aloud will help you to feel more confident and communicate clearly in the interview. Be able to describe your useful skills in layman's terms in case your interviewer is not an expert in the field.

Example

• SITUATION: When I worked at the state library, many of the books were not filed correctly.

• TASK: I was in charge of shelving books on three floors.

• ACTION: I designed and proposed a new employee training method to my boss. I then presented the new method to the library assistants at the next staff meeting and everyone contributed ideas for the new training on shelving.

• RESULT: After that meeting, there were fewer misplaced books, and customers asked fewer questions about finding missing books.

Participate in Mock Interviews

Practice the interview process to improve your communication and overcome nervousness and anxiety.

I would go so far as to interview for jobs that you don't even want just to practice. You should be able to work on your demeanor and confidence level if you know going into the interview it isn't a job that you even want. Try new things here and see what kind of response you can get. When you don't have to worry about getting the job, you can focus on the fundamentals of being an interviewee.

Mock interviews will help you as well. You can do them with a friend or family member or in a mirror. You do whatever you have to do in order to get the job. This may sound like sort of an odd thing to have to do but you won't think it odd when you get the job because you were prepared. Mock interviews will help you get a feel for the interviewing process and become very comfortable with it. It is also an opportunity to create a personality in your head that you can tap into whenever you are in this type of situation. Being a good interviewee is not about how smart you are, it's about how trained you are and how comfortable you are. Believe me when I tell you that you're comfort level will increase exponentially with the more training you have. Practice verbalizing how your background, skills and abilities fit the job you are interviewing for.

Behavior Based Interviews

Behavioral based interviews and questions have become standard practice.

• Recruiters ask for detailed descriptions on how you handled yourself in certain tasks and situations.

• The premise is that past behavior predicts future performance.

Themes for these types of questions include:

• Disagreements and conflicts with coworkers

• Innovative solutions to problems

• Qualities of a team leader and qualities of a team member

• Meeting or failing to meet deadlines

• Responding to criticism from a superior, co-worker, or classmate

• Persuading someone to accept your idea or concept

• Seeing a problem as an opportunity

• Adapting to a wide variety of people, situations, and/or environments

First Impressions

First impressions are lasting ones. Often they are made even before the interview starts, during the application process.

• Voice messages may be the employer's first impression of you.

- The message on your answering machine or voice messaging should be courteous and professional.

- Inform everyone who may answer the telephone that employment calls may come at any time. If you feel your roommates or members of household are unreliable, consider listing a message or cell phone number. Be sure to manage your cell phone calls appropriately.

• Any time you interact with a potential employer or anyone on their staff, imagine that they are evaluating you.

• Be respectful in the way you dress and the way you act.

• Be positive, upbeat and professional when corresponding in person, by mail, phone or email.

• The person answering your questions or taking your application may be the CEO sitting in for the receptionist on a break. You never know!

Dress professionally for the position

• Research industry expectations regarding attire. This could be simply walking through the lobby of the workplace to observe how employees dress.

• Being dressed a little more formally than your Interviewer is acceptable. It shows respect for them, the position, and the company.

• Get plenty of sleep the night before. Your physical appearance will be at its best when you are alert and rested.

• Avoid perfumes and cologne.

Plan ahead to be on time

• Map your route to the interview site.

• Know where to park/how to enter building.

• Plan to arrive 10-15 minutes early.

Introduce yourself politely to the receptionist.

• Introduce yourself to the receptionist and tell them the purpose of visit, and the interviewer's name.

• Thank the receptionist for assistance.

• The receptionist is one of the first employees of the company you will meet. While receptionists may not be making hiring decisions, they will certainly mention their impressions to the interviewer.

Greet the interviewer cordially

• Greet your interviewer using Mr., Ms. or Mrs.

• Shake their hand.

• Tell the interviewer your name.

• Wait to be offered a seat before sitting.

• Relax yourself to appear friendly and be memorable.

Expect small talk

• Engage in the conversation, be responsive and take initiative.

• Do not worry if the conversation catches you off guard, the interviewer may be testing you to see how you react under pressure. Try to relax and respond naturally.

Many interviewers will begin the interview with casual conversation. This is a prelude to the interview where they examine your responses for qualities the company seeks.

The Interview

Your goal in an interview is to show and tell your best qualities to the interviewer.

The interviewer's goal is to evaluate you on different criteria than just skill.

Points to Include in the Interview

• How you fit the job qualifications

• Why you want the job

• Why you want to work for the organization

• What you can contribute to the employer

• What you have learned about yourself and your work

More Tips

• Relate your background and accomplishments to the employer's needs.

• Do not talk about what was wrong with past jobs or past employers.

• Be sincere, positive, and honest with your answers.

• Have your resume and/or portfolio with you in a professional looking folder.

• Avoid mentioning financial concerns or personal problems.

How will you be evaluated?

Once the official part of an interview begins, interviewers will carefully listen and evaluate your responses. In addition to your knowledge about the job and interaction styles, they may look for the following qualities.

- How well do you understand the job and meet its qualifications?

- What skills do you use when interacting with others?

- How mentally alert and responsible are you?

- Can you draw proper inferences and conclusions during the course of the interview?

- Do you demonstrate a degree of intellectual depth when communicating, or is your thinking shallow and lacking depth?

- Have you used good judgment and common sense regarding your life planning up to this point?

- What is your capacity for problem solving?

- How well do you respond to stress and pressure?

Refrain from reciting memorized answers

• Present yourself as interested and naturally enthusiastic about the job, not rehearsed and flat.

• Research the position and organization to fit your skills to the job.

• Formulate concise answers.

Maintain proper body language.

• Sit up straight and look alert.

• Avoid fidgeting.

• Smile when appropriate.

• Maintain eye contact when being asked questions.

• Be aware of your tone of voice. Keep it energetic and avoid monotone answers.

Body language says more about an individual than their words. Match your body language to the impression you want to make.

Be prepared to ask questions

• Prepare 3-5 questions ahead of time.

• Ask about the duties of the job early so you can target your answers to the position.

• Pay attention to an employer's body language and watch how they react to your questions.

• Some employers may start the interview by asking whether you have any questions. Others will tell you that they have set aside time at the end for questions. Others might be comfortable with you asking questions throughout the interview.

If the interview is not going smoothly, don't panic.

• Some interviewers might test you to see how you handle stress.

• Stay positive.

• Ask your interviewer to repeat anything you do not understand so you can gather your thoughts.

Expect the Unexpected

Sometimes questions are asked simply to see how you react.

• Pause briefly.

• Consider the question.

• Give a natural response.

During the interview, you may be asked some unusual questions. Surprise questions could range from, "Where do you see yourself in 5 years" to "If you could live in any time period, which one would it be and why?"

These are not the kind of questions you can prepare for in advance, but your reaction and response will be evaluated by the employer.

The Closing Is Important

Concluding the interview

• Remain enthusiastic and courteous.

• Ask questions.

• Prepare questions ahead of time to help you decide if the position is suitable for you.

• Leave the interviewer(s) with three things that you would like them to remember about you.

This is also an opportunity to give additional information about your background that you think is important to the position and that was not covered in the interview.

Questions to consider asking at the close of the interview

• What do you want the person in this position to accomplish within the first three months?

• Are there are any important skills needed for the job that have not been covered in the interview?

• What is the time frame for making the hiring decision?

Questions to avoid

• What is the starting salary?

• What are the vacation plans, company benefits, or other perks of the job?

• Wait for the interviewer to introduce these subjects. The best time to talk about salary is after you have been offered the job. You are then in a much better position to negotiate.

The conclusion of the interview

• This is usually indicated when the interviewer stands up.

• Shake hands and thank him/her for considering you.

• During the interview or shortly after, write down the name(s) of the interviewer(s) so you won't forget.

Follow Up

• Thank your interviewer for their time before leaving.

• Send a thank you note via email or hand deliver within two days. For examples, see page 30.

The goal of an interview is to leave a positive impression. Remind the interviewer of your interest, but avoid being annoying.

CHAPTER 2: LET ME SHARE WITH YOU HOW I GOT STARTED

When I was first starting out as a developer, I remember how excited I was at the mere thought of having any company interested in me. As time went on and I moved from one company to the next, my salary grew almost exponentially and in a very short period of time.

The first developer job I ever had, my salary was $32,000 per year and I was extremely excited! $16 per hour to do what I love to do was amazing. Six months went by and even though I loved my job, I happened to see a posting for another position at a startup company in Phoenix, Arizona and decided to apply for it. It was a simple HTML developer position. They didn't even require me to be an expert. If I remember correctly, the job description said that I should have "some" knowledge of HTML. Keep in mind it was at a time when HTML was less trivial to know than it is today.

Needless to say, I did the interview and amazingly enough, I got the job. I didn't find out until afterwards that the job paid $64,000 per year! That was a 2 fold increase in my salary in the first 6 months of being a developer! I was ecstatic! You have to believe me when I tell you that this is an anomaly. You will see later in the book that I am a huge believer in finding out the salary or rate before you even get to the interview.

The company was amazing. Every benefit you could possibly imagine came with the job. From free gym memberships to free food and soda all day long, there seemed to be no end. I mean who doesn't love and I mean LOVE free food and soda?! We had lunch and dinner catered from nice restaurants and even kegs of beer brought in every Friday! This was the life and I was as happy as could be.

Fast-forward six more months. My friend Bill sends me an email with a job description that a local company is hiring for. It's a contract position with a company for 6 months with the possibility of extension. The pay is $50 per hour on w2 plus benefits. The job description stated that they wanted someone who had at least a few years of experience with Visual Basic and Desktop Applications development. I had neither. However, I had some knowledge of Visual Basic and was teaching myself the language from a book called "Learn Visual Basic in 21 Days" that I bought for cheap online.

I decide to go in and interview just for the heck of it. Nothing ventured, nothing gained and fortune favors the bold kind of thing. In the interview, I know they are asking me fairly simple technical questions, none of which I answered correctly and all of which was a huge disaster. I left the interview with my spirit broken and headed directly for 31 flavors to drown my sorrows.

The next day I'm back at my job just as happy as could be and grateful for even having the job as I sit eating free Snickers bars and soda. I go to check my email and see an email from the interviewer the company I just interviewed with that reads:

"Greg, thanks for coming in. We have decided that you are a good fit for this position and would like to know when

*you could start? The sooner the better. -
David"*

Um, I don't know what just happened and I have to tell you that my first reaction was that the email is a joke on me because no one could have interviewed any worse than I did nor have less technical ability per the job description.

Now I start calculating what $50 per hour is as compared to my current $64,000 per year salary and it turns out $50 per hour is about $100,000 per year! My jaw drops and frankly I must have blacked out because I don't even remember sending the email back stating how pleased I was that they wanted me and that I could start in 2 weeks, no problem. I packed up all the stuff at my desk, sent my letter of resignation in to my boss and never looked back.

As a side note, that startup company which had received millions of dollars of venture capital to the tune of about 30 million dollars and which had no business plan and no way to really make money went under 2 weeks after I left. I remember talking to my boss just a week before I left and telling him that I cannot believe this company is seemingly doing so well when their only product generates no income whatsoever. I wasn't any kind of business expert buy I figured it was only common sense that at some point you would at least need a product or service which you could make money off of. I say seemingly because who would be giving away so many benefits and perks to their employees unless they were doing really well? Well, it turns out, management wasn't very bright and I guess a less than bright person would also give away benefits and perks when they were making no money. Lesson learned.

So let's look at the timeline here. My first year as a developer I start out making $32,000 per year and as excited as can be. Six months goes by and I have already doubled my income to $64,000 per year. Six more months goes by and my salary has gone up 156.25% to $100,000 per year.

Think it ends there? Think again. Just 4 short months go by and I decide that it is time to start my own consulting business and go find my own clients. I do as much research as possible on how to start my own company and even what kind of company I should start (LLC, S-Corp, C-Corp). After all was said and done, I started an LLC because it was fast, simple and cost virtually nothing to start or maintain in the state of Arizona. My first client was received through word of mouth who basically claimed I was a genius developer and a great guy to boot. My per hour rate? $250 per hour working 40 hour weeks and being my own boss. A 500% increase in salary. I was raking it in, kicking ass and taking names.

Keep in mind the economy at the time was ripe for this kind of rate and businesses seemed to have no end to their cash reserves. The hype to get their business online drove the need to hire good developers who could get the job done and companies were willing to pay top dollar in order to do it.

Luckily I have always had one true asset about my personality that made all of this possible. The ability to read manuals no matter how large they were in 1 sitting. I absolutely despise reading books for leisure. I always have. There is just something about reading a book for fun that irks me and I could never truly pinpoint what that was other than to say, I hate wasting my time for something just to get "fun" as my reward. I am a true Alpha male. I always need to be learning something new or honing my skills, increasing my technical acuity and striving to be the better version of me. Manuals were a way to learn something new, brush up on skills, have more knowledge, and for me, that was the best reward I could receive for my time. 500 page manual on Python? No problem, I'll be done by the end of the day and amazingly enough will retain enough of it to be functional. Sure I didn't memorize the whole thing but I could enough of the gist to actually start getting work done. By the end of the first week I was coding with the best of them. This is how it's always been for me. If I don't know something, I'll go out and learn it, as quickly as possible. I'll try and master it and the best one can be at it.

Between the age of 25 and 30 my net worth went from negative $22,000 racked up on my credit cards to $500,000+ net worth and thoughts of retiring by the age of 32. (I really thought that I just needed 1 million dollars to my name and no debt to retire with. I lived very simply. I found out later that 1 million might not be enough.)

CHAPTER 3: THE ART OF SALARY NEGOTIATION

This section is incredibly important. It will make the difference between you getting $60,000 per year versus $100,000 per year just by changing your mindset. Your self-confidence, self-worth and perceived confidence will sell the best version of you for the most money every time.

Employers hardly ever make their best offer first, and candidates who negotiate their salary generally earn more than those who don't.

Tip: People who at least attempt to ask for a higher salary are perceived more positively, since they're demonstrating the skills the company wants to hire them for.

Here's a step-by-step guide to negotiating your best salary yet:

Do Your Research

Before you go for an interview, you should find out what the market rates are for the job you're looking for. There are salary surveys available online, and if you're dealing with a recruitment agency, your consultant should be able to advise you on the salary range for the position you're interviewing for.

Check online job boards and see what companies are offering for a particular city and area of expertise. I find that general reports on income by professional are grossly inaccurate and misleading. You need to see first-hand what companies are willing to pay. Chances are, the companies that do not post a salary or hourly rate are hiding the fact that they pay way too little. If there is no rate or salary, send them an email and apply whether you are interested or not and ask them what the rate or salary is just so you have a point of reference. The more information you have the better you will be at determining your own self-worth.

Also think about what you want from the job, both in terms of the job itself and in terms of remuneration. This will help you appear more self-assured during the interview and salary negotiation process. The more specific your demands are the better you are perceived and received by the employer.

Psychologically, you are perceived in an entirely different light when you come into an interview with an agenda and knowing exactly what you want out of the job. It demonstrates decisiveness, vision and forethought.

Talk Money Early

Tip: You should always ask about compensation before any interview.

While we all want to earn more when we change jobs, no employer wants to hire someone whose only motivation to change jobs is a higher salary but at the same time, your time is valuable and going in to an interview for 4 hours only to find out it pays way less than you would even remotely find acceptable is a waste of your time and the companies time. Make sure you know exactly what the pay or pay range is up front.

So, how do you answer the inevitable interview question, "What salary are you looking for?"

This is where your homework becomes invaluable. Hopefully, you'll know the market rates for the type of a position you're looking for. It's better to give a range rather than a specific number — you don't want to give a salary that's perhaps lower than the employer is looking to pay, but you don't want to price yourself out of the market, either.

Emphasize that you're primarily interested in finding the right job for you, and salary isn't your main consideration.

Some recruiters have WAY more latitude than they let on.

The typical recruiter almost always has the ability to make the final decision on your compensation package. After you negotiate with them, they will need to go back and confirm the package with a hiring manager or another supervisor.

In other words, the recruiter is going to sell you to the hiring manager. It's up to them to communicate why you deserve a higher salary. You want their support because they are going to need to sell you.

You can help the recruiter out by giving them justification for the items you are asking for and by not coming across as greedy or egotistical.

The single biggest mistake that most candidates make when comes to salary negotiation is telling the recruiter what they would be willing to accept.

Most candidates don't like being pressured, so they simply blurt out a number they are willing to take — but you should never be the first one to name a number.

One way to avoid this common mistake is to ask about the salary range the very first time you meet a recruiter or hiring manager.

If it is not enough than be nice and give clear reasons for the compensation you are requiring. You're not battling against them. You're working with them.

I have worked with some honest recruiters in the past and I have worked with some less than reputable ones and take my word that you need to run when you smell a rat.

I remember taking a position for a company well under my normal rate just because I needed work fast and the job description made it sound very easy with very little responsibility. I went back and forth with the recruiter trying to squeeze as much out of the rate as possible before finally accepting. I ended up with a rate that was $65 per hour and believe me it was a fight to the end to get this much. The recruiter also let me know that I would receive a sign on bonus if I stayed at least 30 days. This seemed sort of odd since I didn't even ask for it but I was more than willing to accept.

By the third day on the job, my boss let it slip that the company was paying my recruiter $135 per hour! Let's do the math here. The recruiter is paying me $65 per hour and the company using the recruiter is paying the recruiter $135 per hour so the recruiter is making $70 per hour for every single hour I worked. The recruiter is not only scamming me out of money but also scamming the company out of a much more experienced developer who would readily accept $100+ per hour versus $65 per hour. The company just got lucky that they hired me for that lesser rate.

Needless to say, I re-negotiated the terms with the recruiter and was making over $100 per hour which was still far less than what the company was paying the recruiter but I was happier in the end, produced better work and stayed longer because of the additional money.

It is important to research the company and the position a recruiter is hiring for to try and get some semblance of what the position is actually paying. You will most likely receive emails from multiple recruiters for the exact same position and I urge you to respond to all of them with the following statement:

"What is the very best rate for this position?"

I think you will be extremely surprised at the responses you get. The same position will have a dramatic range depending on who the recruiter is. *Example*: I received 10 emails from different recruiters for a Senior Architect position with a company in California and to each I responded asking what the very best rate for the position was. I was floored by the responses I received which were anywhere from $50 per hour to $125 per hour for the exact same position with the exact same job requisition number!

Shop around and find the best recruiter you can. It makes a dramatic difference.

Believe That You CAN Negotiate In This Economy

It's true that it will be easier in some industries than others. In my experience, salary scales in the public sector are usually fixed, and there isn't much room for negotiation. When I make offers in my recruitment job, I take into account the candidate's current salary, the company's salary range for the position, market rates and also what other team members are earning.

If you've been selected as the candidate a company wants to hire, and you have some highly sought skills and experience, you're in an excellent position to negotiate.

Don't Be Afraid to Ask — But Don't Demand, Either

Know what you're worth and don't be afraid to ask for it. No one loses a job offer because they ask for something — however, you can have a job offer pulled because of the way you ask.

It's important that your request is within the ballpark of the salary range, so avoid giving a specific number until the employer is ready to make you an offer. Remember to be enthusiastic, polite and professional during negotiations.

Communicate to your prospective employer through your tone of voice and demeanor that your goal is a win-win solution. If you're too pushy, the employer may get the impression that you're not that interested in the job (or only interested in the money) and withdraw the offer.

Keep Selling Yourself

As you go through the interviewing and negotiating process, remind the employer how they will benefit from your skills and experience. Let's say, for example, that the employer wants to offer $70K, but you're looking for minimum $90K base salary.

Explain how they'd benefit by increasing your compensation. *For example*:

"I realize you have a budget to worry about. However, I believe that with the desktop publishing and graphic design skills I bring to the position, you won't have to hire outside vendors to produce customer newsletters and other publications. That alone should produce far more than $20K in savings a year."

In other words, justify every additional dollar or benefit you request. Remember to do so by focusing on the employer's needs, not yours.

Make Them Jealous

If you're interviewing for other jobs, you might want to tell employers about your offer. This should speed up the interview process. If they know you have another offer, you'll seem more attractive to them, and it might help you negotiate a higher salary.

Ask For a Fair Price

You really need to ensure your requests are reasonable and in line with the current marketplace. A few days ago, I spoke to a candidate for an analyst role who'd asked for a salary of $55K – $60K. Since all analysts at his level (three years of experience) earn between $35K – $40K, this candidate had priced himself out of the process with his unreasonable demands.

However, if the salary offer is below market value, you might want to (gently!) suggest it's in the company's best interest to pay the going rate:

"The research that I've done indicates the going rate for a position such as this is $6K higher than this offer. I'd really love to work for you and I believe I can add a lot of value in this job; however, I can't justify doing so for less than market value. I think if you reevaluate the position and consider its importance to your bottom line, you'll find it's worth paying market price to get someone who can really make an impact quickly."

Negotiate Extras and Be Creative!

If the employer can't offer you the salary you want, think about other valuable options that might not cost as much. You can look at negotiating holiday days (e.g. if new employees must work for six to 12 months before receiving paid holidays, ask that this restriction be waived.), ask for yearly salary reviews or negotiate a sign-on or performance bonus.

Be Confident

Remember to use confident body language and speech patterns. When you make a salary request, don't go on and on, stating over and over again why it's justified. Make your request and offer a short, simple explanation of why that amount is appropriate.

Finally, it's a smart negotiating strategy to ask for a few benefits or perks you don't want that badly. Then you can "give in" and agree to take the job without those added benefits if the employer meets all of your other requests.

Ideally, both parties in a negotiation should come away from the table feeling that they've won. This is especially true when you're dealing with salary negotiations. You want employers to have good feelings about the price paid for your services so that your working relationship begins on a positive note.

Keep Track Of What You Have Done Well

The greatest tool that you have in any interview is proof.

Keep examples of your best work, thank you notes from clients, awards or recognitions, and positive work evaluations. Once you discover what is important to the company and how your skills can meet those needs, you can then use these items as proof of the value that you can provide.

It's a lot easier to get a higher salary when you have proof of why you deserve it.

Don't Take It Personally

Easier said than done? Not with practice. Maybe you'll get what you want. Maybe you won't. Life will move on either way. Most people will never have a negotiation that will make or break their life. Keep it real and don't get emotionally involved. If you ask for more than the job is willing to pay than let them call your bluff and give the job to someone else. It is going to be a numbers game and the more you play the game, the better you will be at it and the more money you will make for the exact same 40 hours a week you put in. Get the most money for your time!

CHAPTER 4: HOW TO BECOME A REMOTE WORKER

There are just three ways to become a telecommuter or work remotely. The first is if the job requirement states that it is a telecommuting position. The second is to convince your boss that should telecommute and the third is to be your own boss so you make the rules and deal only with clients who don't care that you work out of your own office.

As a design project manager at a top Internet marketing firm, Mary loved her job but couldn't stand the commute. When the price of gas soared to over $4 a gallon, she realized she was spending a small fortune getting to and from her office in downtown Los Angeles.

Mary had been with the company for four years and was already working at home one day a week. Now she chanced negotiating a permanent telecommuting arrangement with her boss.

"Because our company has a core value of healthy work-life balance, all of our major software is available remotely, and because we have Internet phone lines I thought my boss might be amenable to it," she says. "When I approached my boss I mentioned my existing productivity working from home and how I felt that we could continue to measure that success while

*telecommuting full-time. I promised to
be available to my clients during normal
business hours and to return to the
office two days a month for meetings or
whenever there was an emergency."*

Mary has never been happier. "I get to work from home and also know I have a secure, reliable job."

Her arrangement isn't unique. Organizations around the world are implementing telework with enthusiasm. According to a 2014 study by the American Electronics Association, 47 million Americans already telecommute at least one day a week. BT, a leading provider of communications solutions, hired its first home worker in 1986; today more than 70% of BT's employees benefit from flexible working. The company estimates that it has saved at least $500 million and has improved its productivity by between 15% and 31%.

How do you determine if telecommuting is for you? Michael Randall, a productivity expert, says the best candidates are people who are disciplined and self-motivated: "When your boss says, 'Here's a project, figure it out by this deadline,' do you get it done? Can you stay focused despite distractions and see a task through to completion?" She also says you need to be naturally organized and skilled at time management.

*"People who work from home should be
able to schedule realistically and
prioritize correctly."*

If you think you fit the bill, your first step in making telecommuting a reality is to talk with someone in human resources to find out just how your organization's flexible work policy works. Don't despair if there's no official policy in place. There may be others in your department who are telecommuting successfully, and if you have established a high level of trust with your manager, broaching the issue won't be unreasonable.

To make the argument for telecommuting, prepare a written proposal that puts the organization first and addresses, upfront, the issues you know your boss will be concerned about. The key is to present teleworking as a benefit to the employer. I was once offered a contracting position in which I explained that I could get the same amount of work done in three-quarters of the time from my own office—without the usual interruptions that come with working in a room full of people. It would also be one fewer desk, phone and computer they had to provide and one more notch in their belt as an earth-friendly employer that does what it can to keep cars off the road.

Your proposal should detail how you'll set up your home office, and it should assure your manager that you will have a clean, quiet and child-free work environment in which to complete your duties. Your boss will want to know that you have a fast Internet connection, a dedicated phone number and all the necessary supplies.

Suggest a trial period for the telecommuting arrangement after which you and your manager can evaluate how it's working. Once you're off and running, make a conscious effort to show your boss that you're cutting expenses and getting more done faster. Make sure you're always accessible via e-mail and cellphone during the business day, and report often on where projects stand, so your boss can easily keep tabs on you.

Telecommuting shouldn't mean you never see the inside of the office building again. If you supervise other employees, or make presentations about your initiatives, or are a key participant in team meetings, show up in person as often as you can. Telecommuting must not compromise the critical workplace relationships you've spent time and energy building.

If you're currently job hunting and want to get into a telework situation right at the start, you can turn to a variety of websites that list such positions. FlexJobs.com, for example, is a low-cost subscription service that identifies and screens legitimate telecommuting jobs. Just be aware that telework positions tend to be much more competitive, so your résumé should detail a history of independent work that produced stellar results.

When searching job boards online, you will want to use keywords like "Remote, Virtual or telecommute" in order to find these kind of jobs. I find more often than not the work "Remote" is in ton of job descriptions that are not remote jobs but deal with remote teams because of all of the outsourcing collaboration that is happening.

Also keep in mind that most remote positions pay less and are usually salary based as opposed to hourly but that doesn't mean you can't inquire about the position and ask if it can be done on a contract basis. Be sure to send your references and a job history that includes all of the remote work you have done in the past.

CHAPTER 5: VB.NET INTERVIEW QUESTIONS AND ANSWERS

What are namespaces and how they are used?

The namespace keyword is used to declare a scope that contains a set of related objects. You can use a namespace to organize code elements and to create globally unique types.

What is a constructor?

A constructor is a class member executed when an instance of the class is created. The constructor has the same name as the class. It can be overloaded via different method signatures.

What is the GAC, and where is it located?

The GAC is the Global Assembly Cache. Shared assemblies reside in the GAC. This allows applications to share assemblies instead of having the assembly distributed with each application. Versioning allows multiple assembly versions to exist in the GAC. Applications can specify version numbers in their respective configuration file.

How are assemblies managed in the GAC?

The gacutil.exe command line tool is used to manage the GAC.

What does immutable mean as pertaining to vb strings?

Immutable means string values cannot be changed once they have been created. Any modification to a string value results in a completely new string instance.

What is a reason for having strings be immutable?

Strings will never get a race conditions because of corruption.

What is "DLL Hell", and how does the GAC solve it?

"DLL Hell" describes the difficulty in managing versioning of dynamic linked libraries on a system. This includes multiple copies of a DLL, different versions, and so forth. When a DLL (or assembly) is loaded in .NET, it is loaded by name, version and certificate. The assembly contains all of this information via its metadata. The GAC provides the solution, as you can have multiple versions of a DLL side-by-side.

How are methods overloaded?

Methods are overloaded via different signatures (number of parameters and types). Thus, you can overload a method by having different data types, different number of parameters, or a different order of parameters.

How do you prevent a class from being inherited?

The NotInheritable keyword prohibits a class from being inherited.

What does the keyword AddHandler do?

Associates an event with an event handler at runtime.

What is the execution entry point for a vb.net console application?

The Main procedure. This Main procedure is present in every executable vb.net application. This includes any console application, Windows desktop application or Windows service application.

What if we have more classes with Main procedure?

The class that defines the Main procedure is termed an Application object. However, it is possible that we have more than one class that contains a Main method. We can set which classes Main procedure will be used as the entry point via the Startup Object drop down list box, located under the Application tab of the Visual Studio project properties editor. This value is saved in the corresponding .SUO (Solution User Options) file.

What does the Widening keyword indicate?

Indicates that a conversion operator (CType) converts a class or structure to a type that can hold all possible values of the original class or structure.

Why is the Main procedure static?

Static members are scoped to the class level (rather than the object level) and can thus be invoked without the need to first create a new class instance. The Main procedure is static because it is available to run when your program starts and as it is the entry point of the program it runs without creating an instance of the class. In other words, static functions exist before a class is instantiated so static is applied to the main entry point.

What are String() args in Main procedure? What are there use?

The String() arguments may contain any number of command line arguments which are then available within the Main procedure.

What is the access modifier declaration of the Main procedure and why?

The Main procedure must be marked private. The reason behind this is so other applications cannot invoke the entry point. The Main procedure cannot be declared public.

What does WithEvents specify?

Specifies that one or more declared member variables refer to an instance of a class that can raise events. When a variable is defined using WithEvents, you can declaratively specify that a method handles the variable's events using the Handles keyword.

What is the return value of Main procedure?

The return value of Main procedure is void (indicates no return value) by default.

What is use of the integer return value in the Main procedure?

The integer return value of the Main procedure indicates whether an error occurred. If the Main procedure executes successfully then it will return 0 (default value even if it defined as void). If the Main procedure executes unsuccessfully then the return value will be -1.

How do you escape strings in vb?

Escaping is never allowed in vb, so there is no need to escape the backslash.

What are some differences between a struct and a class?

Structs cannot be inherited. Structs are passed by value and not by reference. Structs are stored on the stack not the heap. The result is better performance with structs.

What does yield do?

When you use the yield keyword in a statement, you indicate that the method, operator, or get accessor in which it appears is an iterator. Using yield to define an iterator removes the need for an explicit extra class.

What are some restrictions to using yield?

A yield return statement can't be located in a try-catch block. A yield return statement can be located in the try block of a try-finally statement. A yield break statement can be located in a try block or a catch block but not a finally block.

Can you have more than one yield return in the same iterator?

Yes, you can use more than one yield statement in the same iterator.

What is early binding and how does it work?

The compiler performs a process called binding when an object is assigned to an object variable. An object is early bound when it is assigned to a variable declared to be of a specific object type. Early bound objects allow the compiler to allocate memory and perform other optimizations before an application executes

What are the advantages to early binding?

You should use early-bound objects whenever possible, because they allow the compiler to make important optimizations that yield more efficient applications. Early-bound objects are significantly faster than late-bound objects and make your code easier to read and maintain by stating exactly what kind of objects are being used. Another advantage to early binding is that it enables useful features such as automatic code completion and Dynamic Help because the Visual Studio integrated development environment (IDE) can determine exactly what type of object you are working with as you edit the code. Early binding reduces the number and severity of run-time errors because it allows the compiler to report errors when a program is compiled.

What are dynamic objects in vb.net?

Dynamic objects provide another way, other than the Object type, to late bind to an object at run time. A dynamic object exposes members such as properties and methods at run time by using dynamic interfaces that are defined in the System.Dynamic namespace. You can use the classes in the System.Dynamic namespace to create objects that work with data structures that do not match a static type or format.

What is reflection?

Reflection provides objects (of type Type) that describe assemblies, modules and types. You can use reflection to dynamically create an instance of a type, bind the type to an existing object, or get the type from an existing object and invoke its methods or access its fields and properties. If you are using attributes in your code, reflection enables you to access them.

What is a partial class?

A class which can span multiple source files for the ease of development.

Can we override a constructor?

No

What is the use of TryCast operator?

Instead of direct casting TryCast first tests for source type and then casts it. It returns Nothing if cast fails.

What is a singleton?

A singleton is a design pattern used when only one instance of an object is created and shared; that is, it only allows one instance of itself to be created. Any attempt to create another instance simply returns a reference to the first one. Singleton classes are created by defining all class constructors as private. In addition, a private static member is created as the same type of the class, along with a public static member that returns an instance of the class.

What is boxing?

Boxing is the process of explicitly converting a value type into a corresponding reference type. Basically, this involves creating a new object on the heap and placing the value there. Reversing the process is just as easy with unboxing, which converts the value in an object reference on the heap into a corresponding value type on the stack. The unboxing process begins by verifying that the recipient value type is equivalent to the boxed type. If the operation is permitted, the value is copied to the stack.

What are lambda expressions and what is a simple syntax example?

A lambda expression is an anonymous function that you can use to create delegates or expression tree types. By using lambda expressions, you can write local functions that can be passed as arguments or returned as the value of function calls. Lambda expressions are particularly helpful for writing LINQ query expressions.

An example:

```
DIM FUNC1 AS FUNC(OF INTEGER, INTEGER) = FUNCTION(VALUE AS INTEGER)

        RETURN VALUE + 1

END FUNCTION
```

What are extension methods?

Extension methods enable you to "add" methods to existing types without creating a new derived type, recompiling, or otherwise modifying the original type. Extension methods are a special kind of static method, but they are called as if they were instance methods on the extended type. For client code written in C# and Visual Basic, there is no apparent difference between calling an extension method and the methods that are actually defined in a type.

Name the two emergent roles involved when using delegates?

Broadcasters and subscribers.

What is a thread?

VB.net supports parallel execution of code through multithreading. A thread is an independent execution path, able to run simultaneously with the other threads.

What is the difference between vb.net Thread.Sleep() and Join()?

Sleep causes the current thread to sleep for the specified amount of time. Join will wait (block) the current thread until the referenced thread completes.

What are mutexes?

You can use a Mutex object to provide exclusive access to a resource. The Mutex class uses more system resources than the Monitor class, but it can be marshaled across application domain boundaries, it can be used with multiple waits, and it can be used to synchronize threads in different processes.

What are abandoned mutexes?

If a thread terminates without releasing a Mutex, the mutex is said to be abandoned. This often indicates a serious programming error because the resource the mutex is protecting might be left in an inconsistent state.

What types of mutexes can be created in vb.net?

Mutexes are of two types: local mutexes and named system mutexes. If you create a Mutex object using a constructor that accepts a name, it is associated with an operating-system object of that name. Named system mutexes are visible throughout the operating system and can be used to synchronize the activities of processes. You can create multiple Mutex objects that represent the same named system mutex, and you can use the OpenExisting method to open an existing named system mutex.

A local mutex exists only within your process. It can be used by any thread in your process that has a reference to the local Mutex object. Each Mutex object is a separate local mutex.

What is the significance of Finalize method in .NET?

.NET Garbage collector does almost all clean up activity for your objects. But unmanaged resources (example: Windows API created objects, File, Database connection objects, COM objects, etc.) are outside the scope of .NET Framework. We have to explicitly clean our resources. For these types of objects, .NET Framework provides Object.Finalize method, which can be overridden and clean up code for unmanaged resources can be put in this section?

Why is it preferred to not use finalize for clean up?

The problem with finalize is that garbage collection has to make two rounds in order to remove objects which have finalize methods.

What is the use of Dispose method?

Dispose method belongs to 'IDisposable' interface. If any object wants to release its unmanaged code, the best way to go about this is to implement IDisposable and override the Dispose method of IDisposable interface. Once your class has exposed the Dispose method, it is the responsibility of the client to call the Dispose method to do the cleanup.

How do I force the Dispose method to be called automatically, as clients can forget to call Dispose method?

Call the Dispose method in Finalize method and in the Dispose method, suppress the finalize method using GC.SuppressFinalize. This is the best way we do clean our unallocated resources and to not get the hit of running the Garbage collector twice.

What is an interface and what is an abstract class? Please expand by examples of using both. Explain why.

Answer 1

In an interface class, all methods are abstract without implementation whereas in an abstract class, methods can be defined. In interface, no accessibility modifiers are allowed. An abstract class may have accessibility modifiers. Interface and abstract class are basically a set of rules which you have to follow in case you are using them (inheriting them).

Answer 2

Abstract classes are closely related to interfaces. They are classes that cannot be instantiated, and are frequently either partially implemented, or not at all implemented. One key difference between abstract classes and interfaces is that a class may implement an unlimited number of interfaces, but may inherit from only one abstract (or any other kind of) class. A class that is derived from an abstract class may still implement interfaces. Abstract classes are useful when creating components because they allow you to specify an invariant level of functionality in some methods, but leave the implementation of other methods until a specific implementation of that class is needed. They also version well, because if additional functionality is needed in derived classes, it can be added to the base class without breaking code.

Answer 3

Abstract Classes

An abstract class is the one that is not used to create objects. An abstract class is designed to act as a base class (to be inherited by other classes). Abstract class is a design concept in program development and provides a base upon which other classes are built. Abstract classes are similar to interfaces. After declaring an abstract class, it cannot be instantiated on its own, it must be inherited. Like interfaces, abstract classes can specify members that must be implemented in inheriting classes. Unlike interfaces, a class can inherit only one abstract class. Abstract classes can only specify members that should be implemented by all inheriting classes.

Answer 4

An interface looks like a class, but has no implementation. They're great for putting together plug-n-play like architectures where components can be interchanged at will. Think Firefox Plug-in extension implementation. If you need to change your design, make it an interface. However, you may have abstract classes that provide some default behavior. Abstract classes are excellent candidates inside of application frameworks.

Answer 5

One additional key difference between interfaces and abstract classes (possibly the most important one) is that multiple interfaces can be implemented by a class, but only one abstract class can be inherited by any single class.

Some background on this: C++ supports multiple inheritance, but vb.net does not. Multiple inheritance in C++ has always been controversial, because the resolution of multiple inherited implementations of the same method from different base classes is hard to control and anticipate. VB.net decided to avoid this problem by allowing a class to implement multiple interfaces, which do not contain method implementations, but restricting a class to have at most a single parent class. Although this can result in redundant implementations of the same method when different classes implement the same interface, it is still an excellent compromise.

Another difference between interfaces and abstract classes is that an interface can be inherited by an abstract class, but no class, abstract or otherwise, can be inherited by an interface.

Answer 6

An abstract class is a special kind of class that cannot be instantiated. So the question is why we need a class that cannot be instantiated? An abstract class is only to be sub-classed (inherited from). In other words, it only allows other classes to inherit from it but cannot be instantiated. The advantage is that it enforces certain hierarchies for all the subclasses. In simple words, it is a kind of contract that forces all the subclasses to carry on the same hierarchies or standards.

An interface is not a class. It is an entity that is defined by the word Interface. An interface has no implementation; it only has the signature or in other words, just the definition of the methods without the body. As one of the similarities to Abstract class, it is a contract that is used to define hierarchies for all subclasses or it defines specific set of methods and their arguments. The main difference between them is that a class can implement more than one interface but can only inherit from one abstract class. Since vb.net doesn't support multiple inheritance, interfaces are used to implement multiple inheritance.

What is polymorphism?

One of the fundamental concepts of object oriented software development is polymorphism. The term polymorphism (from the Greek meaning "having multiple forms") in OO is the characteristic of being able to assign a different meaning or usage to something in different contexts - specifically, to allow a variable to refer to more than one type of object.

What is vb.net?

VB.net is an object oriented, type safe and managed language that is compiled by .Net framework to generate Microsoft Intermediate Language.

What are the types of comment in vb.net with examples?

1. Single line represented by ' or REM.

2. XML Comments ('").

Can multiple catch blocks be executed?

No, Multiple catch blocks can't be executed. Multiple catch blocks can be declared. Once the proper catch code executed, the control is transferred to the finally block and then the code that follows the finally block gets executed.

What is the difference between Public and Static?

Specifies that one or more declared local variables are to continue to exist and retain their latest values after termination of the procedure in which they are declared.

The Public (Visual Basic) keyword in the declaration statement specifies that the elements can be accessed from code anywhere in the same project, from other projects that reference the project, and from any assembly built from the project. You can use Public only at module, interface, or namespace level. This means you can declare a public element at the level of a source file or namespace, or inside an interface, module, class, or structure, but not in a procedure.

What is an object?

An object is an instance of a class through which we access the methods of that class. "New" keyword is used to create an object. A class that creates an object in memory will contain the information about the methods, variables and behavior of that class.

What are constructors?

A constructor is a member function in a class that has the same name as its class. The constructor is automatically invoked whenever an object class is created. It constructs the values of data members while initializing the class.

What is Jagged Arrays?

The array which has elements of type array is called jagged array. The elements can be of different dimensions and sizes. We can also call jagged array as Array of arrays.

What are the two ways to pass arguments to a procedure?

In Visual Basic, you can pass an argument to a procedure by value or by reference. This is known as the passing mechanism, and it determines whether the procedure can modify the programming element underlying the argument in the calling code. The procedure declaration determines the passing mechanism for each parameter by specifying the ByVal (Visual Basic) or ByRef (Visual Basic) keyword.

What is the use of using statement in vb.net?

The using block is used to obtain a resource and use it and then automatically dispose of when the execution of block completed.

What is serialization?

When we want to transport an object through a network then we have to convert the object into a stream of bytes. The process of converting an object into a stream of bytes is called Serialization. For an object to be serializable, it should inherit the ISerialize Interface.

De-serialization is the reverse process of creating an object from a stream of bytes.

Can "Me" be used within a static method?

We can't use "Me" in a static method because we can only use static variables/methods in a static method. "Me" refers to a specific object reference.

What is difference between constant and read-only?

You use the const keyword to declare a constant field or a constant local. This keyword specifies that the value of the field or the local variable is constant, which means that it can't be modified. The static modifier is not allowed in a constant declaration. A constant expression is an expression that can be fully evaluated at compile time. Therefore, the only possible values for constants of reference types are string and null.

The ReadOnly keyword differs from the const keyword. A const field can only be initialized at the declaration of the field. A read only field can be initialized either at the declaration or in a constructor. Therefore, read only fields can have different values depending on the constructor used. A const field is a compile-time constant whereas the read only field can be used for run-time constants.

What are value types and reference types?

- All numeric data types

- Boolean , Char, and Date

- All structures, even if their members are reference types

- Enumerations, since their underlying type is always SByte, Short, Integer, Long, Byte, UShort, UInteger, or ULong

Every structure is a value type, even if it contains reference type members. For this reason, value types such as Char and Integer are implemented by .NET Framework structures.

You can declare a value type by using the reserved keyword, for example, Decimal. You can also use the New keyword to initialize a value type. This is especially useful if the type has a constructor that takes parameters. An example of this is the Decimal(Int32, Int32, Int32, Boolean, Byte) constructor, which builds a new Decimal value from the supplied parts.

A reference type contains a pointer to another memory location that holds the data. Reference types include the following:

- String
- All arrays, even if their elements are value types
- Class types, such as Form
- Delegates

A class is a reference type. For this reason, reference types such as Object and String are supported by .NET Framework classes. Note that every array is a reference type, even if its members are value types.

Since every reference type represents an underlying .NET Framework class, you must use the New Operator (Visual Basic) keyword when you initialize it. The following statement initializes an array.

What does the NotInheritable keyword do?

When applied to a class, the NotInheritable modifier prevents other classes from inheriting from it. You can also use the NotInheritable modifier on a method or property that overrides a virtual method or property in a base class. This enables you to allow classes to derive from your class and prevent them from overriding specific virtual methods or properties.

What is method overloading?

Method overloading is creating multiple methods with the same name with unique signatures in the same class. When we compile, the compiler uses overload resolution to determine the specific method to be invoke.

What is the difference between Array and ArrayList?

In an array, we can have items of the same type only. The size of the array is fixed. An ArrayList is similar to an array but it doesn't have a fixed size.

Can a private virtual (Overridable) method be overridden?

No, because they are not accessible outside the class.

Describe the accessibility modifier "Protected Friend".

Protected Friend variables/methods are accessible from the classes that are derived from this parent class within the same assembly.

What are the differences between System.String and System.Text.StringBuilder classes?

System.String is immutable. When we modify the value of a string variable then a new memory is allocated to the new value and the previous memory allocation released. System.StringBuilder was designed to have concept of a mutable string where a variety of operations can be performed without allocation separate memory location for the modified string.

What's the difference between the System.Array.CopyTo() and System.Array.Clone()?

Using Clone() method, we creates a new array object containing all the elements in the original array. When using the CopyTo() method, all elements of the existing array are copied into another existing array. Both the methods perform a shallow copy.

How can we sort the elements of the array in descending order?

Using Sort() methods followed by Reverse() method.

What are circular references?

Circular reference is situation in which two or more resources are interdependent on each other causes the lock condition and make the resources unusable.

What are generics in vb.net.NET?

Generics are used to make reusable code classes to decrease the code redundancy, increase type safety and performance. Using generics, we can create collection classes. Generics promotes the usage of parameterized types.

What is an object pool in .NET?

An object pool is a container having objects ready to be used. It tracks the object that is currently in use, total number of objects in the pool. This reduces the overhead of creating and re-creating objects.

What are the commonly used types of exceptions in .Net?

• ArgumentException

• ArgumentNullException

• ArgumentOutOfRangeException

• ArithmeticException

• DivideByZeroException

• OverflowException

• IndexOutOfRangeException

• InvalidCastException

• InvalidOperationException

• IOEndOfStreamException

• NullReferenceException

• OutOfMemoryException

• StackOverflowException

What are custom Exceptions?

User defined exceptions.

What are delegates?

Delegates are same are function pointers in C++ but the only difference is that they are type safe unlike function pointers. Delegates are required because they can be used to write much more generic type safe functions.

What is the syntax to inherit from a class in vb.net?

The Inherits keyword.

What is the base class in .net from which all the classes are derived from?

System.Object

What is the difference between method overriding and method overloading?

In method overriding, we change the method definition in the derived class in order to change the method behavior. Method overloading is creating a method with the same name within the same class having different method signatures.

What does Shadows mean?

Specifies that a declared programming element re-declares and hides an identically named element, or set of overloaded elements, in a base class.

What are the different ways a method can be overloaded?

Methods can be overloaded using different data types for parameter, different order of parameters, and different number of parameters.

Why can't you specify the accessibility modifier for methods inside the interface?

In an interface, we have virtual methods that do not have method definition. All the methods are there to be overridden in the derived class. That is why they must be marked as Public.

How can we set class to be inherited, but prevent the method from being overridden?

Declare the class as Public and make the method NotInheritable to prevent it from being overridden.

What happens if the inherited interfaces have conflicting method names?

The interface method that gets implemented is up to you as the method is inside your own class. There may be problems when the method from different interfaces expect different data, but as far as the compiler is concerned it is up to you.

What are Modules?

A Module statement defines a reference type available throughout its namespace. A module (sometimes called a standard module) is similar to a class but with some important distinctions. Every module has exactly one instance and does not need to be created or assigned to a variable. Modules do not support inheritance or implement interfaces. Notice that a module is not a type in the sense that a class or structure is — you cannot declare a programming element to have the data type of a module.

What is the lifetime of a Module?

A module has the same lifetime as your program. Because its members are all Shared, they also have lifetimes equal to that of the program.

What is the difference between a Struct and a Class?

Structs are value-type variables and classes are reference types. Structs stored on the stack, causes additional overhead but faster retrieval. Structs cannot be inherited.

How to use nullable types in .Net?

Value types can take either their normal values or a null value. Such types are called nullable types.

How we can create an array with non-default values?

We can create an array with non-default values using Enumerable.Repeat.

What's a multicast delegate?

A delegate having multiple handlers assigned to it is called multicast delegate. Each handler is assigned to a method.

What are indexers in vb.net?

Indexers are known as smart arrays in vb.net. It allows the instances of a class to be indexed in the same way as an array.

What is difference between the "throw" and "throw ex" in .NET?

"Throw" statement preserves original error stack whereas "throw ex" have the stack trace from their throw point. It is always advised to use "throw" because it provides more accurate error information.

What are vb.net attributes and their significance?

VB.net provides developers a way to define declarative tags on certain entities e.g. Class, method etc. are called attributes. The attribute's information can be retrieved at runtime using Reflection.

What is the difference between a direct cast and CType?

A direct cast is used to convert the type of an object that requires the run-time type to be the same as the specified type. CType is used for conversion where the conversion is defined between the expression and the type.

Is vb.net code managed or unmanaged code?

VB.net is managed code because common language runtime can compile VB.net code to Intermediate language.

What does the AndAlso operator do?

Performs short-circuiting logical conjunction on two expressions.

What are some characteristics of vb.net?

1. Simple

2. Type safe

3. Flexible

4. Object oriented

5. Compatible

6. Consistent

7. Interoperable

8. Modern

What are the different categories of inheritance in vb.net?

1. Single inheritance: Contains one base class and one derived class.

2. Hierarchical inheritance: Contains one base class and multiple derived classes of the same base class.

3. Multilevel inheritance: Contains a class derived from a derived class.

4. Multiple inheritance: Contains several base classes and a derived class.

Can you inherit multiple interfaces?

Yes. Multiple interfaces may be inherited in vb.net.

Define scope?

Scope refers to the region of code in which a variable may be accessed.

Can you use unreserved keywords names?

You can use unreserved keyword names for your programming elements. However, doing this is not recommended, because it can make your code hard to read and can lead to subtle errors that can be difficult to find.

What are some examples of modifiers in vb.net?

- Shadows
- MustInherit
- NotInheritable
- Inherits
- Implements
- ReadOnly

- New

How can you reallocate storage space for an array variable?

ReDim

What are the types of access modifiers in vb.net?

- Public

- Protected

- Private

- Friend

- Protected Friend

Where are the types of arrays in vb.net?

- Single-Dimensional

- Multidimensional

- Jagged arrays

What is the difference between Object and Instance?

An instance of a user-defined type is called an object. We can instantiate many objects from one class. An object is an instance of a class.

What does REM do?

Creates a single line remark or comment.

What is a class destructor?

A destructor is called for a class object when that object passes out of scope or is explicitly deleted. A destructor as the name implies is used to destroy the objects that have been created by a constructor. Like a constructor, the destructor is a member function whose name is the same as the class name but is prefaced by a tilde.

Every property must have a Set property procedure unless the property is marked?

ReadOnly

What is the use of enumerated data type?

An enumerated data type is another user defined type which provides a way for attaching names to numbers thereby increasing comprehensibility of the code. The Enum keyword automatically enumerates a list of words by assigning them values 0,1,2, and so on.

What is encapsulation?

The wrapping up of data and functions into a single logical unit is known as encapsulation. Encapsulation contains and hides information about an object, such as internal data structures and code.

Does vb.net support multiple class inheritance?

No.

Give a brief explanation of what covariance and contravariance do?

Covariance and contravariance enable implicit reference conversion for array types, delegate types, and generic type arguments. Covariance preserves assignment compatibility and contravariance reverses it.

What does the Stop statement do?

It suspends execution. You can place Stop statements anywhere in procedures to suspend execution. Using the Stop statement is similar to setting a breakpoint in the code.

Unlike End, Stop does not close any files or clear any variables, unless it is encountered in a compiled executable (.exe) file.

What is an Enum?

The Enum keyword is used to declare an enumeration, a distinct type that consists of a set of named constants called the enumerator list.

How do you refer to a base class in vb?

Using the MyBase specifier.

What is the difference between Private and Public keyword?

The Private keyword is the default access level and most restrictive among all other access levels. It gives least permission to a type or type member. A private member is accessible only within the body of the class in which it is declared.

The Public keyword is most liberal among all access levels, with no restrictions to access what so ever. A public member is accessible not only from within, but also from outside, and gives free access to any member declared within the body or outside the body.

What is the use of using statement in vb.net?

The using statement is used to obtain a resource, execute a statement, and then dispose of that resource.

What is Authentication and Authorization and how do they differ?

Authentication is the process of identifying users. Authentication is identifying/validating the user against the credentials (username and password).

Authorization performs after authentication. Authorization is the process of granting access to those users based on identity.

Authorization allowing access of specific resource to user.

What is a base class?

A class declaration may specify a base class by following the class name with a colon and the name of the base class. Omitting a base class specification is the same as deriving from type object.

What are the different types of statements supported in vb.net?

- Block statements
- Declaration statements
- Expression statements
- Selection statements
- Iteration statements
- Jump statements
- Try catch statements
- Checked and unchecked
- Lock statement

What are the different types of Caching?

- Output Caching: stores the responses from an asp.net page.
- Fragment Caching: Only caches/stores the portion of page (User Control)
- Data Caching: is Programmatic way to Cache objects for performance.

What are methods?

A method is a member that implements a computation or action that can be performed by an object or class. Static methods are accessed through the class. Instance methods are accessed through instances of the class.

What are fields?

A field is a variable that is associated with a class or with an instance of a class.

What are events?

An event is a member that enables a class or object to provide notifications. An event is declared like a field except that the declaration includes an event keyword and the type must be a delegate type.

What are literals? What type do literals have?

Literals are value constants assigned to variables in a program. VB.net supports several types of literals are:

- Integer literals

- Real literals

- Boolean literals

- Single character literals

- String literals

- Backslash character literals

What are the types of errors?

- Syntax error

- Logic error

- Runtime error

What is the difference between the Break and Continue statement?

The Break statement is used to terminate the current enclosing loop or conditional statements in which it appears. We have already used the break statement to come out of switch statements.

The Continue statement is used to alter the sequence of execution. Instead of coming out of the loop like the break statement did, the continue statement stops the current iteration and simply returns control back to the top of the loop.

What is a code group?

A code group is a set of assemblies that share a security context.

What are the different types of variables in VB.net?

- static variables

- instance variable

- value parameters

- reference parameters

- array elements
- output parameters
- local variables

Is vb.net is object oriented?

Yes, vb.net is an OO langauge in the tradition of Java and C++.

What is meant by operators in vb.net?

An operator is a member that defines the meaning of applying a particular expression operator to instances of a class. Three kinds of operators can be defined: unary operators, binary operators, and conversion operators. All operators must be declared as public and static.

What is a parameterized type?

A parameterized type is a type that is parameterized over another value or type.

What is the use of GoTo statement?

The GoTo statement is also included in the vb.net language. This GoTo can be used to jump from inside a loop to outside. But jumping from outside to inside a loop is not allowed.

What is the difference between console and window application?

A console application, which is designed to run at the command line with no user interface. A Windows application, which is designed to run on a user's desktop and has a user interface.

What is the use of Return statement?

The Return statement is associated with procedures (methods or functions). On executing the return statement, the system passes the control from the called procedure to the calling procedure. This return statement is used for two purposes:

1. To return immediately to the caller of the currently executed code

2. To return some value to the caller of the currently executed code.

What is the difference between Array and LinkedList?

Array is a simple sequence of numbers which are not concerned about each others positions. They are independent of each others positions. adding, removing or modifying any array element is very easy. Compared to arrays,linked list is a complicated sequence of numbers.

Does vb.net have a throws clause?

No, unlike Java, vb.net does not require the developer to specify the exceptions that a method can throw.

Does vb.net support optional parameters?

You can specify that a procedure parameter is optional and no argument has to be supplied for it when the procedure is called. Optional parameters are indicated by the Optional keyword in the procedure definition.

Can you override private virtual methods?

No, private methods are not accessible outside the class.

Are use of exceptions in vb.net recommended?

Yes, exceptions are the recommended error handling mechanism in .NET Framework.

Is vb.net object oriented?

Yes, vb.net is an OO language in the tradition of java and C++.

What is smart navigation?

The cursor position is maintained when the page gets refreshed due to the server side validation and the page gets refreshed.

What is the difference between Const and ReadOnly?

Both are meant for constant values. A Const field can only be initialized at the declaration of the field. A ReadOnly field can be initialized either at the declaration or.

Does vb.net have a throws clause?

No, unlike Java, vb.net does not require (or even allow) the developer to specify the exceptions that a method can throw.

What are the different ways a method can be overloaded?

Different parameter data types, different number of parameters, different order of parameters.

Do events have return type?

No, events do not have return type.

What is an event?

An event is an action performed based on another method of the program.

An event is a delegate type class member that is used by an object or a class to provide a notification to other objects that an event has occurred.

An event can be declared with the help of the event keyword.

What is an identifier?

Identifiers are nothing but names given to various entities uniquely identified in a program.

What is a literal in vb?

A literal is a value that is expressed as itself rather than as a variable's value or the result of an expression, such as the number 3 or the string "Hello". A constant is a meaningful name that takes the place of a literal and retains this same value throughout the program, as opposed to a variable, whose value may change.

When Option Infer is Off and Option Strict is On, what must you do?

You must declare all constants explicitly with a data type.

What is meant by data encapsulation?

Data encapsulation, also referred to as data hiding, is the mechanism whereby the implementation details of a class are kept hidden from the user. The user can only perform a restricted set of operations on the hidden members of the class by executing special functions called methods.

Can you override private virtual methods?

No. Private methods are not accessible outside the class.

What is the main difference between a subprocedure and a function?

Subprocedures do not return a value, while functions do.

What is nested class?

Nested classes are classes defined within other classes. A nested class is any class whose declaration occurs within the body of another class or interface.

Is String a Value Type or Reference Type in vb.net?

String is an object (Reference Type).

Can a Class or a Struct have multiple constructors?

Yes, a class or a struct can have multiple constructors. Constructors in VB.net can be overloaded.

Can you create an instance of an interface?

No, you cannot create an instance of an interface.

Can an Interface contain fields?

No, an Interface cannot contain fields.

What is the main use of delegates in vb.net?

Delegates are mainly used to define call back methods.

What is the difference between Shadowing and Overriding?

Overriding redefines only the implementation while shadowing redefines the whole element. In overriding derived classes can refer the parent class element by using "Me" keyword, but in shadowing you can access it by "MyBase".

Can events have access modifiers?

Yes, you can have access modifiers in events. You can have events with the protected keyword, which will be accessible only to inherited classes. You can have private events only for objects in that class.

How can we suppress a finalize method?

GC.SuppressFinalize()

Which method will you call to start a thread?

Start

What is a Generic?

Generics help us to create flexible strong type collection. Generics basically separate the logic from the data type in order maintain better reusability, better maintainability etc.

What are the different types of polymorphism?

- Compile time Polymorphism
- Run time Polymorphism

What is the difference between compile time polymorphism and run time polymorphism?

Compile time Polymorphism also known as method overloading. Method overloading means having two or more methods with the same name but with different signatures.

Run time Polymorphism also known as method overriding. Method overriding means having two or more methods with the same name, same signature but with different implementation.

Which namespace enables multithreaded programming in XML?

System.Threading

What is a basic difference between the while loop and do while loop in vb.net?

The while loop tests its condition at the beginning, which means that the enclosed set of statements run for zero or more number of times if the condition evaluates to true. The do while loop iterates a set of statements at least once and then checks the condition at the end.

What is the difference between class and an Interface?

Abstract classes can have implementations for some of its members, but the interface can't have implementation for any of its members.

Interfaces cannot have fields whereas an abstract class can have fields.

An interface can inherit from another interface only and cannot inherit from an abstract class, whereas an abstract class can inherit from another abstract class or another interface.

A class can inherit from multiple interfaces at the same time, whereas a class cannot inherit from multiple classes at the same time.

Abstract class members can have access modifiers whereas interface members cannot have access modifiers.

What is the difference between an abstract method & virtual method?

An Abstract method does not provide an implementation and forces overriding to the deriving class (unless the deriving class also an abstract class), whereas the virtual method has an implementation and leaves an option to override it in the deriving class. Thus Virtual method has an implementation & provides the derived class with the option of overriding it. Abstract method does not provide an implementation & forces the derived class to override the method.

What are nullable types?

Nullable types are instances of the System.Nullable(Of T) struct. A nullable type can represent the correct range of values for its underlying value type, plus an additional null value.

Can you box a nullable type?

Objects based on nullable types are only boxed if the object is non-null.

What is LINQ?

Language-Integrated Query (LINQ) is the name for a set of technologies based on the integration of query capabilities directly into the C# language (also in Visual Basic and potentially any other .NET language). With LINQ, a query is now a first-class language construct, just like classes, methods, events and so on.

What is a mutable type?

A type whose instance data, fields and properties, can be changed after the instance is created.

What is refactoring?

Code refactoring is the process of restructuring existing computer code – changing the factoring – without changing its external behavior. Refactoring improves nonfunctional attributes of the software. Advantages include improved code readability and reduced complexity to improve source code maintainability, and create a more expressive internal architecture or object model to improve extensibility.

What are preprocessor directives?

Preprocessor directives, such as #define and #ifdef, are typically used to make source programs easy to change and easy to compile in different execution environments. Directives in the source file tell the preprocessor to perform specific actions.

What kind of things get stored in the memory stack or heap?

We have four main types of things we'll be putting in the Stack and Heap as our code is executing: Value Types, Reference Types, Pointers, and Instructions.

Where do reference types get stored?

The heap

Is xml case-sensitive?

Yes

When a value type is declared within a method, where does it get stored in memory?

The stack.

What kind of things can you make generic c#?

Methods, classes, structures, or interfaces.

What is an accessible member?

A member that can be accessed by a given type. An accessible member for one type is not necessarily accessible to another type.

What is an anonymous method?

An anonymous method is a code block that is passed as a parameter to a delegate.

What are the advantages of get and set properties?

They allow us to hide class members.

What does CLS stand for?

Common Language Specification.

CHAPTER 6: ASP.NET QUESTIONS AND ANSWERS

How does output caching work in ASP.NET?

Output caching is a powerful technique that increases request/response throughput by caching the content generated from dynamic pages. Output caching is enabled by default, but output from any given response is not cached unless explicit action is taken to make the response cacheable.

To make a response eligible for output caching, it must have a valid expiration/validation policy and public cache visibility. This can be done using either the low-level OutputCache API or the high-level @ OutputCache directive. When output caching is enabled, an output cache entry is created on the first GET request to the page. Subsequent GET or HEAD requests are served from the output cache entry until the cached request expires.

The output cache also supports variations of cached GET or POST name/value pairs.

The output cache respects the expiration and validation policies for pages. If a page is in the output cache and has been marked with an expiration policy that indicates that the page expires 60 minutes from the time it is cached, the page is removed from the output cache after 60 minutes. If another request is received after that time, the page code is executed and the page can be cached again. This type of expiration policy is called absolute expiration - a page is valid until a certain time.

What are different methods of session maintenance in ASP.NET?

There are three types:

1. In-process storage (Default location for session state)

2. Session State Service

3. Microsoft SQL Server

What is the Session State Service and what is the benefit of using it?

As an alternative to using in-process storage for session state, ASP.NET provides the ASP.NET State Service. The State Service gives you an out-of-process alternative for storing session state that is not tied quite so closely to ASP. NET's own process.

There are two main advantages to using the State Service. First, it is not running in the same process as ASP.NET, so a crash of ASP.NET will not destroy session information. Second, the stateConnectionString that's used to locate the State Service includes the TCP/IP address of the service, which need not be running on the same computer as ASP.NET. This allows you to share state information across a web garden (multiple processors on the same computer) or even across a web farm (multiple servers running the application). With the default in-process storage, you can't share state information between multiple instances of your application.

What does the "EnableViewState" property do? Why would I want it on or off?

Enable ViewState turns on the automatic state management feature that enables server controls to re-populate their values on a round trip without requiring you to write any code. This feature is not free however, since the state of a control is passed to and from the server in a hidden form field. You should be aware of when ViewState is helping you and when it is not.

***What is the difference between Server.Transfer and Response.Redirect and w**hy would I choose one over the other?*

Server.Transfer(): The client is not aware of a page change as no headers are passed back. Transfer to the new page is done on the server side. Data can be persisted across the pages using Context.Item collection, which is one of the best ways to transfer data from one page to another keeping the page state alive.

Response.Redirect(): The web server will send back a redirect command to the client to request the new url.

Context.Items loses its' persistence when navigating to destination page. In earlier versions of IIS, if we wanted to send a user to a new Web page, the only option we had was Response.Redirect. While this method does accomplish our goal, it has several important drawbacks. The biggest problem is that this method causes each page to be treated as a separate transaction. Besides making it difficult to maintain your transactional integrity, Response.Redirect introduces some additional headaches. First, it prevents good encapsulation of code. Second, you lose access to all of the properties in the Request object.

What are custom controls and user controls?

Custom Controls are controls generated as compiled code (Dlls), those are easier to use and can be added to toolbox. Developers can drag and drop controls to their web forms. Attributes can be set at design time. We can easily add custom controls to Multiple Applications (If Shared Dlls), if they are private then we can copy to dll to bin directory of web application and then add reference and can use them.

User Controls are very much similar to ASP include files, and are easy to create. User controls can't be placed in the toolbox and dragged – dropped from it. They have their design and code behind. The file extension for user controls is ascx.

What are page directives?

The first line of an ASP.NET page is the page directive; you will find it on all ASP.NET pages. These directives are instructions for the page. It begins with the @Page directive and continues with the various attributes available to this directive.

It's unreasonable to expect a candidate to know all of these attributes, but a few popular ones include the following.

- AutoEventWireup: Indicates whether page events are autowired.

- CodeBehind: The name of the compiled class associated with the page.

- Debug: Indicates whether the page is compiled in debug mode (includes debug symbols).

- EnableTheming: Indicates whether themes are used on the page.

- EnableViewState: Indicates whether view state is maintained across pages.

- ErrorPage: Specifies a target URL to be used when unhandled exceptions occur.

- Language: Indicates the language used when compiling inline code on the page.

- Trace: Signals whether tracing is enabled on the page.

What is a master page?

A master page is a template for one or more web forms. The master page defines how the page will be laid out when presented to the user, with placeholders for content. The MasterPageFile Page Directive in a content page's header is one way to assign a master page. The content pages rely solely on content and leave layout to the master page. ASP.NET merges the content with the master page layout when the content page is requested by a user.

What is the code behind feature of ASP.NET?

The code behind feature divides ASP.NET page files into two files where one defines the user interface (.aspx), while the other contains all of the logic or code (.aspx.cs for C# and .aspx.vb for VB.NET). These two files are glued together with page directives like the following line, which ties the page to the specific code behind class.

```
<%@    Page    language="c#"    Codebehind="UICode.cs"
Inherits="Library.UICode" %>
```

What are ASHX files?

ASP.NET Web handler files have an .ashx file extension. Web handlers work just like .aspx files except you don't have to deal with the browser interface, thus no worrying about presentation. Web handlers are generally used to generate content dynamically like returning XML or an image. Web handlers use the IHttpHandler interface with the ProcessRequest() method invoked when the handler is requested. Web handlers are simpler than pages (fewer events and wiring), so they are ideal for performance-critical applications.

How does PostBack work?

PostBack is basically the ASP.NET submitting a form to it -- it posts back to the current URL. The JavaScript __doPostBack function is placed on the page (look at the source within the browser) to facilitate. PostBack uses ViewState to remember controls and data. The IsPostBack property of the ASP.NET page allows you to determine if the loading of the page is the result of a postback event; this is done in the Page_Load event.

How can you pass values between ASP.NET pages?

There are numerous ways to accomplish this task; the option you choose depends on the environment. The oldest way to approach it is via the QueryString (i.e., passing values via URL); this is also one of the least secure ways because users can easily see the data and could possibly hack the site/page by changing parameter values. Next, you can use HTTP POST to pass values; these are available via a collection within the ASP.NET page. More specific to ASP.NET is the use of Session state, which makes information available to all pages within the ASP.NET application. Another approach is using public properties on the source page and accessing these properties on the target page. Also, you can use the PreviousPage property of the current page to access control information on the referring page. The last two require the source, and target pages are within the same ASP.NET application.

What are ASP.NET Server controls?

ASP.NET includes a number of built-in server controls that are the foundation of its Web programming model. They have various properties to control their behavior and appearance. These controls provide an event model where events are handled on the server (whereas HTML controls are handled in the client). Server controls have the ability to maintain state (via ViewState) across requests, and they can automatically detect the browser. With these controls, you will see the RunAt attribute (RunAt="Server") that signals its processing will be done on the server.

What is View State?

Basically, view state is how ASP.NET Web pages persists data across requests. It handles data that must be preserved between postbacks, and you can use it to store page-specific data. By default, view state is enabled on a page and its controls. This can be a problem as the amount of data and controls on a page increases resulting in more data for ASP.NET to maintain. This is accomplished via the hidden __VIEWSTATE field on a form (look at the page source in a browser), so more data in this field means a slower load time and slower overall processing, as it has to be posted to the server each time. You can limit the size of the data in view state by disabling controls that do not need to be persisted via the EnableViewState property.

How can you prevent tampering of view state?

View state can be encrypted to address security concerns.

What is the global.asax file?

The global.asax file is an optional piece of an ASP.NET application. It is located in the root of the application directory structure. It cannot be directly loaded or requested by users. It provides a place to define application- and session-wide events. You can define your own events, but it does contain default Application events like when the application starts Application_Start and ends with Application_End. The same is true for Session events (Session_Start and Session_End).

How can you loop through all controls on an ASP.NET Web form?

You can easily traverse all controls on a form via the Web Form's Controls collection. The GetType method can be used on each control to determine its type and how to work with it. Now, it gets tricky because the form contains a tree of controls; that is, some controls are contained within others (think of a Table). You would have to recursively loop through the controls to make sure everything is processed.

What is a web.config file? Machine.config?

The web.config is the basic configuration file for ASP.NET applications. It utilizes an XML format. It is used to define application settings, connection strings, and much more. These files can appear in multiple directories, and they are applied in a top-down approach; that is, configuration files apply to their container directory as well as all directories below it, but the configuration files in lower directories can override those in parent directories. This provides a way to granularly apply settings. The machine.config file contains ASP.NET settings for all of the applications on the server -- it is at the top of the configuration file hierarchy, thus web.configs can override it.

CHAPTER 7: OBJECT ORIENTED INTERVIEW QUESTIONS

The following are interview questions that are conceptual in nature and deal with object oriented programming in a general way. Some questions will not necessarily apply to c# but are good to know moving forward.

What is OOP?

Object-oriented programming (OOP) is a programming paradigm that represents concepts as "objects" that have data fields (attributes that describe the object) and associated procedures known as methods. Objects, which are usually instances of classes, are used to interact with one another to design applications and computer programs.

Write basic concepts of OOPS?

• Abstraction.

• Encapsulation.

• Inheritance.

• Polymorphism.

What is a class?

A class is simply a representation of a type of object. It is the blueprint/ plan/ template that describe the details of an object.

What is an object?

Object is termed as an instance of a class, and it has its own state, behavior and identity.

What is Encapsulation?

Encapsulation is the packing of data and functions into a single component. The features of encapsulation are supported using classes. It allows selective hiding of properties and methods in a class by building an impenetrable wall to protect the code from accidental corruption. Encapsulation, inheritance, and polymorphism are the three pillars of object-oriented programming.

What is Polymorphism?

In programming languages and type theory, polymorphism (from Greek, "many, much" and "form, shape") is the provision of a single interface to entities of different types. A polymorphic type is a type whose operations can also be applied to values of some other type, or types.

What is Inheritance?

Inheritance is a concept where one class shares the structure and behavior defined in another class. If inheritance applied on one class is called Single Inheritance, and if it depends on multiple classes, then it is called multiple Inheritance.

Define what a constructor is?

Constructor is a method used to initialize the state of an object, and it gets invoked at the time of object creation. Rules for a constructor are:

• Constructor Name should be same as class name.

• Constructor must have no return type.

Define a destructor?

Destructor is a method which is automatically called when the object is made of scope or destroyed. Destructor name is also same as class name but with the tilde symbol before the name.

What is an Inline function?

Inline function is a technique used by the compilers and instructs to insert complete body of the function wherever that function is used in the program source code.

What is a virtual function?

Virtual function is a member function of class and its functionality can be overridden in its derived class. This function can be implemented by using a keyword called virtual, and it can be given during function declaration.

Virtual function can be achieved in C++, and it can be achieved in C language by using function pointers or pointers to function.

What is friend function?

Friend function is a friend of a class that is allowed to access to Public, private or protected data in that same class. If the function is defined outside the class cannot access such information.

Friend can be declared anywhere in the class declaration, and it cannot be affected by access control keywords like private, public or protected.

What is function overloading?

Function overloading is defined as a normal function, but it has the ability to perform different tasks. It allows creation of several methods with the same name which differ from each other by type of input and output of the function.

What is operator overloading?

Operator overloading permits user-defined operator implementations to be specified for operations where one or both of the operands are of a user-defined class or struct type.

What is an abstract class?

An abstract class is a class which cannot be instantiated. Creation of an object is not possible with abstract class, but it can be inherited. An abstract class can contain only Abstract method.

What is a ternary operator?

Ternary operator is said to be an operator which takes three arguments. Arguments and results are of different data types, and it is depends on the function. Ternary operator is also called as conditional operator.

What are the different categories of inheritance in OOP?

1. Single inheritance: Contains one base class and one derived class.

2. Hierarchical inheritance: Contains one base class and multiple derived classes of the same base class.

3. Multilevel inheritance: Contains a class derived from a derived class.

4. Multiple inheritance: Contains several base classes and a derived class.

What are different types of arguments?

• A parameter is a variable used during the declaration of the function or subroutine and arguments are passed to the function and it should match with the parameter defined. There are two types of Arguments.

• Call by Value – Value passed will get modified only inside the function, and it returns the same value whatever it is passed it into the function.

• Call by Reference – Value passed will get modified in both inside and outside the functions and it returns the same or different value.

What is super keyword?

In c++. The super keyword is used to invoke overridden method which overrides one of its superclass methods. This keyword allows to access overridden methods and also to access hidden members of the superclass. It also forwards a call from a constructor to a constructor in the superclass.

What is method overriding?

Method overriding is a feature that allows sub class to provide implementation of a method that is already defined in the main class. This will overrides the implementation in the superclass by providing the same method name, same parameter and same return type.

What is an interface?

An interface is a collection of abstract method. If the class implements an inheritance, and then thereby inherits all the abstract methods of an interface.

What is exception handling?

Exception is an event that occurs during the execution of a program. Exceptions can be of any type – Run time exception, Error exceptions. Those exceptions are handled properly through exception handling mechanism like try, catch and throw keywords.

What are tokens?

A token is recognized by a compiler and it cannot be broken down into component elements. Keywords, identifiers, constants, string literals and operators are examples of tokens.

Even punctuation characters are also considered as tokens – Brackets, Commas, Braces and Parentheses.

What is the difference between overloading and overriding?

Member overloading means creating two or more members on the same type that differ only in the number or type of parameters but have the same name.

The override modifier is required to extend or modify the abstract or virtual implementation of an inherited method, property, indexer, or event.

What is the difference between class and an object?

An object is an instance of a class. Objects hold any information, but classes don't have any information. Definition of properties and functions can be done at class and can be used by the object.

Class can have sub-classes, and an object doesn't have sub-objects.

What is an abstraction?

Abstraction is a good feature of OOP showing only necessary details to the consumer of an object. It shows only necessary details for an object, not the inner details of an object.

What are access modifiers?

Access modifiers determine the scope of the method or variables that can be accessed from other various objects or classes. There are 5 types of access modifiers, and they are as follows:

- Private

- Protected

- Public

- Friend

- Protected Friend

What are sealed modifiers?

When applied to a class, the sealed modifier prevents other classes from inheriting from it. In the following example, class B inherits from class A, but no class can inherit from class B.

How can we call the base method without creating an instance?

Use a static method on the base class. Inherit from that class then use the base Keyword from the derived class.

What is the difference between new and override?

The new modifier instructs the compiler to see the method with an entirely different method signature and bypass the rules of polymorphism and overrides in c#. The override modifier helps to override the base class function.

What are the various types of constructors?

• Default Constructor – With no parameters.

• Parametric Constructor – With Parameters. Create a new instance of a class and also passing arguments simultaneously.

• Copy Constructor – Which creates a new object as a copy of an existing object.

What is early and late binding?

Early binding refers to assignment of values to variables during design time whereas late binding refers to assignment of values to variables during run time.

What is the "this" keyword in c#?

The "this" keyword refers to an objects current instance of itself.

What is the default access modifier in a class?

In c#, the default access modifier of a class is private by default.

What is pure virtual function?

In c++. a pure virtual function is a function which can be overridden in the derived class but cannot be defined. A virtual function can be declared as pure by using the operator =0.

What is dynamic or run time polymorphism?

Dynamic or Run time polymorphism is also known as method overriding in which call to an overridden function is resolved during run time, not at compile time. It means having two or more methods with the same name, same signature but with different implementation.

Are parameters required for constructors?

No

What does the keyword virtual mean?

It means, we can override the method.

Can static methods use non static members?

No.

What are base class, sub class and super class?

• Base class is the most generalized class, and it is said to be a root class.

• Sub class is a class that inherits from one or more base classes.

• Super class is the parent class from which another class inherits.

What is static and dynamic binding?

• Binding is nothing but the association of a name with the class. Static binding is a binding in which name can be associated with the class during compilation time and it is also called as early Binding.

• Dynamic binding is a binding in which name can be associated with the class during execution time, and it is also called as Late Binding.

How many instances can be created for an abstract class?

None, you cannot implement an abstract class.

Which OOP concept is used as a re-use mechanism?

Inheritance.

Which OOP concept exposes only necessary information to the calling functions?

Data Hiding / Abstraction

What is a design pattern?

A design pattern is a general reusable solution to a commonly occurring problem within a given context in software design. A design pattern is not a finished design that can be transformed directly into source or machine code. It is a description or template for how to solve a problem that can be used in many different situations. Patterns are formalized best practices that the programmer must implement in the application.

What are examples of different types of patterns?

Structural, creational, behavioral, concurrency.

Name some structural design patterns?

Adapter, Bridge, Composite, Decorator, Façade, Flyweight, Front Controller, Module, Proxy.

Briefly describe the façade design pattern?

Provide a unified interface to a set of interfaces in a subsystem. Facade defines a higher-level interface that makes the subsystem easier to use.

What Inversion of Control (IoC) mean?

Inversion of Control (IoC) means that objects do not create other objects on which they rely to do their work. Instead, they get the objects that they need from an outside source (for example, an xml configuration file).

What does dependency injection (DI) mean?

Dependency Injection (DI) means that IoC is done without the object intervention, usually by a framework component that passes constructor parameters and set properties.

What is meant by a decoupled architecture?

In general, a decoupled architecture is a framework for complex work that allows components to remain completely autonomous and unaware of each other.

CHAPTER 8: MVC QUESTIONS AND ANSWERS

What is MVC (Model View Controller)?

MVC is an architectural pattern which separates the representation and user interaction. It's divided into three broader sections, model, view, and controller. Below is how each one of them handles the task.

1. The view is responsible for the look and feel.

2. Model represents the real world object and provides data to the View.

3. The Controller is responsible for taking the end user request and loading the appropriate Model and View.

What is the difference between ASP.NET MVC and ASP.NET web forms?

ASP.NET Web Forms uses Page controller pattern approach for rendering layout, whereas ASP.NET MVC uses Front controller approach. In case of Page controller approach, every page has its own controller, i.e., code-behind file that processes the request. On the other hand, in ASP.NET MVC, a common controller for all pages processes the requests.

What is the request flow in ASP.NET MVC framework?

Request hits the controller coming from client. Controller plays its role and decides which model to use in order to serve the request further passing that model to view which then transforms the model and generates an appropriate response that is rendered to the client.

What is Routing in ASP.NET MVC?

In case of a typical ASP.NET application, incoming requests are mapped to physical files such as .aspx file. ASP.NET MVC framework uses friendly URLs that more easily describe user's action but are not mapped to physical files.

ASP.NET MVC framework uses a routing engine that maps URLs to controller classes. We can define routing rules for the engine, so that it can map incoming request URLs to appropriate controller

Can you explain the complete flow of MVC?

Below are the steps to control flows in MVC (Model, View, and controller) architecture:

- All end user requests are first sent to the controller.

- The controller depending on the request decides which model to load. The controller loads the model and attaches the model with the appropriate view.

- The final view is then attached with the model data and sent as a response to the end user on the browser.

Is MVC suitable for both Windows and Web applications?

The MVC architecture is suited for a web application than Windows. For Window applications, MVP, i.e., "Model View Presenter" is more applicable. If you are using WPF and Silverlight, MVVM is more suitable due to bindings.

What are the benefits of using MVC?

• Separation of concerns is achieved as we are moving the code-behind to a separate class file. By moving the binding code to a separate class file we can reuse the code to a great extent.

• Automated UI testing is possible because now the behind code (UI interaction code) has moved to a simple .NET class. This gives us opportunity to write unit tests and automate manual testing.

Is MVC different from a three layered architecture?

MVC is an evolution of a three layered traditional architecture. Many components of the three layered architecture are part of MVC.

What are HTML helpers in MVC?

HTML helpers help you to render HTML controls in the view. For instance if you want to display a HTML textbox on the view, below is the HTML helper code.

What is the difference between "HTML.TextBox" vs "HTML.TextBoxFor"?

Both of them provide the same HTML output, "HTML.TextBoxFor" is strongly typed while "HTML.TextBox" isn't. Below is a simple HTML code which just creates a simple textbox with "CustomerCode" as name.

What is routing in MVC?

Routing helps you to define a URL structure and map the URL with the controller.

For instance let's say we want that when a user types "http://localhost/View/ViewCustomer/", it goes to the "Customer" Controller and invokes the DisplayCustomer action. This is defined by adding an entry in to the routes collection using the maproute function. Below is the underlined code which shows how the URL structure and mapping with controller and action is defined.

What is the use of display modes?

View can be changed automatically based on display size, browser type, device type, etc.

Where is the route mapping code written?

The route mapping code is written in the "global.asax" file.

Can we map multiple URL's to the same action?

Yes, you can, you just need to make two entries with different key names and specify the same controller and action.

How can we navigate from one view to another using a hyperlink?

By using the ActionLink method as shown in the below code. The below code will create a simple URL which helps to navigate to the "Home" controller and invoke the GotoHome action.

How can we restrict MVC actions to be invoked only by GET or POST?

Decorate the MVC action with the HttpGet or HttpPost attribute to restrict the type of HTTP calls.

What are the difference between tempdata, viewdata, and viewbag

- Temp data - Helps to maintain data when you move from one controller to another controller or from one action to another action. In other words when you redirect, tempdata helps to maintain data between those redirects. It internally uses session variables.

- View data - Helps to maintain data when you move from controller to view.

- View Bag - It's a dynamic wrapper around view data. When you use Viewbag type, casting is not required. It uses the dynamic keyword internally.

What are partial views in MVC?

Partial view is a reusable view (like a user control) which can be embedded inside other view. For example let's say all your pages of your site have a standard structure with left menu, header, and footer as shown in the image below.

For every page you would like to reuse the left menu, header, and footer controls. So you can go and create partial views for each of these items and then you call that partial view in the main view.

How did you create a partial view and consume it?

When you add a view to your project in Visual Studio you check the "Create partial view" check box.

Once the partial view is created you can then call the partial view in the main view using the Html.RenderPartial method as shown in the below code snippet:

How can we do validations in MVC?

One of the easiest ways of doing validation in MVC is by using data annotations. Data annotations are nothing but attributes which can be applied on model properties.

How to we display validation errors to the client?

In order to display the validation error message we need to use the ValidateMessageFor method which belongs to the Html helper class.

How do you check to see if the Model is valid in a particular controller method?

Check ModelState.IsValid or TryUpdateModel.

Can we display all errors in one go?

Yes, we can; use the ValidationSummary method from the Html helper class.

What are the other data annotation attributes for validation in MVC?

- StringLength

- RegularExpression

- Range

- Compare

How do you add error in the controller to a Model?

AddModelError function.

How can we enable data annotation validation on client side?

It's a two-step process: first reference the necessary jQuery files. The second step is to call the EnableClientValidation method.

What is Razor in MVC?

It's a light weight view engine. Till MVC we had only one view type, i.e., ASPX. Razor was introduced in MVC 3.

Why Razor when we already have ASPX?

Razor is clean, lightweight, and syntaxes are easy as compared to ASPX. For example, in ASPX to display simple time, we need to write:

So which is a better fit, Razor or ASPX?

As per Microsoft, Razor is more preferred because it's light weight and has simple syntaxes.

How can you do authentication and authorization in MVC?

You can use Windows or Forms authentication for MVC.

Then in the controller or on the action, you can use the Authorize attribute which specifies which users have access to these controllers and actions. Below is the code snippet for that. Now only the users specified in the controller and action can access it.

How do you implement Forms authentication in MVC?

Forms authentication is implemented the same way as in ASP.NET. The first step is to set the authentication mode equal to Forms. The loginUrl points to a controller here rather than a page.

We also need to create a controller where we will check if the user is proper or not. If the user is proper we will set the cookie value.

How to implement AJAX in MVC?

You can implement AJAX in two ways in MVC:

1. AJAX libraries
2. jQuery

What is the difference between ActionResult and ViewResult?

• ActionResult is an abstract class while ViewResult derives from the ActionResult class. ActionResult has several derived classes like ViewResult, JsonResult, FileStreamResult, and so on.

• ActionResult can be used to exploit polymorphism and dynamism. So if you are returning different types of views dynamically, ActionResult is the best thing. For example in the below code snippet, you can see we have a simple action called DynamicView. Depending on the flag (IsHtmlView) it will either return a ViewResult or JsonResult.

What are the different types of results in MVC?

There 12 kinds of results in MVC, at the top is the ActionResult class which is a base class that can have 11 subtypes as listed below:

1. ViewResult - Renders a specified view to the response stream

2. PartialViewResult - Renders a specified partial view to the response stream

3. EmptyResult - An empty response is returned

4. RedirectResult - Performs an HTTP redirection to a specified URL

5. RedirectToRouteResult - Performs an HTTP redirection to a URL that is determined by the routing engine, based on given route data

6. JsonResult - Serializes a given ViewData object to JSON format

7. JavaScriptResult - Returns a piece of JavaScript code that can be executed on the client

8. ContentResult - Writes content to the response stream without requiring a view

9. FileContentResult - Returns a file to the client

10. FileStreamResult - Returns a file to the client, which is provided by a Stream

11. FilePathResult - Returns a file to the client

What are ActionFilters in MVC?

ActionFilters help you to perform logic while an MVC action is executing or after an MVC action has executed.

When are Action filters useful?

- Implement post-processing logic before the action happens.

- Cancel a current execution.

- Inspect the returned value.

- Provide extra data to the action.

How can you create action filters?

1. Inline action filter.

2. Creating an ActionFilter attribute.

Can we create our custom view engine using MVC?

Yes, you can create your own custom view engine in MVC.

What is WebAPI?

WebAPI is the technology by which you can expose data over HTTP following REST principles.

What is bundling and minification in MVC?

Bundling and minification helps us improve request load times of a page thus increasing performance.

How does bundling increase performance?

Web projects always need CSS and script files. Bundling helps us combine multiple JavaScript and CSS files in to a single entity thus minimizing multiple requests in to a single request.

So how do we implement bundling in MVC?

Open BundleConfig.cs from the App_Start folder.

How can you test bundling in debug mode?

If you are in a debug mode you need to set EnableOptimizations to true in the bundleconfig.cs file or else you will not see the bundling effect in the page requests.

Explain Areas in MVC?

To accommodate large projects, ASP.NET MVC lets you partition Web applications into smaller units that are referred to as areas. Areas provide a way to separate a large MVC Web application into smaller functional groupings. An area is effectively an MVC structure inside an application. An application could contain several MVC structures (areas).

CHAPTER 9: ENTITY FRAMEWORK QUESTIONS AND ANSWERS

What is entity framework?

ADO.NET entity is an ORM (object relational mapping) which creates a higher abstract object model over ADO.NET components. So rather than getting into dataset, datatables, command, and connection objects as shown in the below code, you work on higher level domain objects like customers, suppliers, etc.

What are the benefits of using EF?

The main and the only benefit of EF is it auto-generates code for the Model (middle layer), Data Access Layer, and mapping code, thus reducing a lot of development time.

What are the different ways of creating these domain / entity objects?

Entity objects can be created in two ways: from a database structure, or by starting from scratch by creating a model.

What is pluralize and singularize in the Entity Framework dialog box?

"Pluralize" and "Singularize" give meaningful naming conventions to objects. In simple words it says do you want to represent your objects with the below naming convention:

• One Customer record means "Customer" (singular).

• Lot of customer records means "Customer's" (plural, watch the "s")

What is the importance of EDMX file in Entity Framework?

EDMX (Entity Data Model XML) is an XML file which contains all the mapping details of how your objects map with SQL tables. The EDMX file is further divided into three sections: CSDL, SSDL, and MSL.

Can you explain CSDL, SSDL and MSL sections in an EDMX file?

• CSDL (Conceptual Schema definition language) is the conceptual abstraction which is exposed to the application.

• SSDL (Storage Schema Definition Language) defines the mapping with your RDBMS data structure.

• MSL (Mapping Schema Language) connects the CSDL and SSDL.

CSDL, SSDL and MSL are actually XML files.

What are T4 templates?

T4 (Text Template Transformation Toolkit) is a template based code generation engine. You can go and write vb.net code in T4 templates (.tt is the extension) files and those vb.net codes execute to generate the file as per the written vb.net logic.

What is the importance of T4 in Entity Framework?

T4 files are the heart of EF code generation. The T4 code templates read the EDMX XML file and generate vb.net behind code. This vb.net behind code is nothing but your entity and context classes.

How can we read records using Entity Framework classes?

In order to browse through records you can create the object of the context class and inside the context class you will get the records.

How can we add, update, and delete using EF?

Create the object of your entity class, add it to the data context using AddObject method, and then call the SaveChanges method.

If you want to update, select the object, make changes to the object, and call AcceptAllChanges.

If you want to delete, call the DeleteObject method.

Why would anyone say Entity Framework runs slow?

By default EF has lazy loading behavior. Due to this default behavior if you are loading a large number of records and especially if they have foreign key relationships, you can have performance issues. So you need to be cautious if you really need lazy loading behavior for all scenarios. For better performance, disable lazy loading when you are loading a large number of records or use stored procedures.

What does lazy loading refer to?

Lazy loading is a concept where we load objects on demand rather than loading everything in one go. Entity Framework has lazy loading behavior by default enabled.

How can we turn off lazy loading?

The opposite of lazy loading is eager loading. In eager loading we load the objects beforehand. So the first thing is we need to disable lazy loading by setting LazyLoadingEnabled to false.

What are POCO classes in Entity Framework?

POCO means Plain Old vb.net Object. When EDMX creates classes, they are cluttered with a lot of entity tags. You can create a simple .NET class and use the entity context object to load your simple .NET classes.

How do we implement POCO in Entity Framework?

To implement POCO is a three step process:

1.Go to the designer and set the code generation strategy to NONE. This step means that you would be generating the classes on your own rather than relying on EF auto code generation.

2. Now that auto generation of code is disabled, create the domain classes manually. Add a class file and create the domain classes.

3. Finally, use the created code in your client as if you were using EF normally.

In POCO classes do we need EDMX files?

Yes, you will still need EDMX files because the context object reads the EDMX files to do the mapping.

What is Code First approach in Entity Framework?

In Code First approach we avoid working with the Visual Designer of Entity Framework. In other words the EDMX file is excluded from the solution. So you now have complete control over the context class as well as the entity classes.

What are the differences between POCO, Code First and simple EF approach?

All these three approaches define how much control you want on your Entity Framework code.

Entity Framework is an OR mapper, it generates a lot of code, it creates your middle tier (Entity), and Data Access layer (Context).

In simple Entity Framework, everything is auto generated and so you need the EDMX XML file as well. POCO is semi-automatic so you have full control on the entity classes but then the context classes are still generated by the EDMX file.

In Code First, you have complete control on how you can create the entity and context classes. Because you are going to manually create these classes, you do not have dependency on the EDMX XML file.

What is optimistic locking and pessimistic locking?

Optimistic Locking

Optimistic Locking is a strategy where you read a record, take note of a version number, timestamp or state of a row and check that change has not happened before you write the record back. When you write the record back you filter the update on the version to make sure it's atomic. (i.e. hasn't been updated between when you check the version and write the record to the disk) and update the version in one hit.

If the record is dirty (i.e. different version to yours) you abort the transaction and the user can re-start it.

This strategy is most applicable to high-volume systems and three-tier architectures where you do not necessarily maintain a connection to the database for your session. In this situation the client cannot actually maintain database locks as the connections are taken from a pool and you may not be using the same connection from one access to the next.

Pessimistic Locking

Pessimistic Locking is when you lock the record for your exclusive use until you have finished with it. It has much better integrity than optimistic locking but requires you to be careful with your application design to avoid Deadlocks. To use pessimistic locking you need either a direct connection to the database (as would typically be the case in a two tier client server application) or an externally available transaction ID that can be used independently of the connection.

In the latter case you open the transaction with the TxID and then reconnect using that ID. The DBMS maintains the locks and allows you to pick the session back up through the TxID. This is how distributed transactions using two-phase commit protocols (such as XA or COM+ Transactions) work.

How can we handle concurrency in Entity Framework?

In EF, concurrency issue is resolved by using optimistic locking. To implement optimistic locking, right click on the EDMX designer and set the concurrency mode to Fixed.

How can we do pessimistic locking in Entity Framework?

We cannot do pessimistic locking using Entity Framework. You can invoke a stored procedure from Entity Framework and do pessimistic locking by setting the isolation level in the stored procedure. But directly, Entity Framework does not support pessimistic locking.

What is client wins and store wins mode in Entity Framework concurrency?

Client wins and store wins are actions which you would like to take when concurrency happens. In store wins / database wins, the data from the server is loaded into your entity objects. Client wins is opposite to stored wins, data from the entity object is saved to the database.

We need to use the Refresh method of the Entity Framework context and provide the RefreshMode enum values.

What are scalar and navigation properties in Entity Framework?

Scalar properties have actual values contained in the entities. Normally a scalar property will map to a database field.

Navigation properties help to navigate from one entity to another entity. Navigation properties are automatically created from the primary and foreign key references.

What are complex types in Entity Framework?

Types containing common properties used across multiple entities. To create a complex type, select the fields which you want to group in a complex type, click on Refactor, and create the complex type.

What's the difference between LINQ to SQL and Entity Framework?

• LINQ to SQL is good for rapid development with SQL Server. EF is for enterprise scenarios and works with SQL Server as well as other databases.

• LINQ maps directly to tables. One LINQ entity class maps to one table. EF has a conceptual model and that conceptual model maps to the storage model via mappings. So one EF class can map to multiple tables, or one table can map to multiple classes.

• LINQ is more targeted towards rapid development while EF is for enterprise level where the need is to develop a loosely coupled framework.

What is the difference between DbContext and ObjectContext?

DbContext is a wrapper around ObjectContext. It is a simplified version of ObjectContext.

As a developer you can start with DbContext as it is simple to use. When you feel that some of the operations cannot be achieved by DbContext, you can then access ObjectContext from DbContext.

CHAPTER 10: WCF QUESTIONS AND ANSWERS

What is SOA?

Service-oriented architecture (SOA) is a software design and software architecture design pattern based on discrete pieces of software providing application functionality as services to other applications. This is known as service-orientation. It is independent of any vendor, product or technology.

What is the difference between Service and Component?

A service can be made up of several components. Usually a service provides one complete feature that is made up by combining different components.

The client doesn't need to know anything about the underlying components. The client will deal directly with the service while the service will be interacting with the components internally.

What are basic steps to create a WCF service?

1. Create Service Contract
2. Expose Endpoints with Metadata
3. Implement Service
4. Consume Service

What are endpoints, address, contracts and bindings?

All communication with a Windows Communication Foundation (WCF) service occurs through the endpoints of the service. Endpoints provide clients access to the functionality offered by a WCF service.

Each endpoint consists of four properties:

1. An address that indicates where the endpoint can be found.

2. A binding that specifies how a client can communicate with the endpoint.

3. A contract that identifies the operations available.

4. A set of behaviors that specify local implementation details of the endpoint.

What are various ways of hosting WCF service?

There are four common ways:

1. Hosting in IIS

2. Hosting in WAS

3. Hosting in a Windows service

4. Hosting in an application (aka "self-hosting")

What are some benefits of hosting a WCF service in IIS?

• Built-in logging, application pool scaling, throttling and configuration of your site

• Built-in features allow for population of context classes with information and state. i.e. HttpContext

• Built-in security features. i.e. Authorization

• Memory recycling features when processes fail or based on time interval.

What is 1difference between BasicHttpBinding and WsHttpBinding?

One of the biggest differences you must have noticed is the security aspect. By default, BasicHttpBinding sends data in plain text while WsHttpBinding sends it in an encrypted and secured manner.

How can we do debugging and tracing in WCF?

You can debug the WCF service as you do with other web application. Configuring tracing is enabled from the web.config.

What is a transaction in WCF?

A transaction is a logical unit of work consisting of multiple activities that need to all succeed or all fail otherwise any work that was done is rolled back. Transaction attributes can be applied to methods within a service contract and implemented within the service definition.

How can we self-host WCF service?

To host a service inside a managed application, embed the code for the service inside the managed application code, define an endpoint for the service either imperatively in code, declaratively through configuration, or using default endpoints, and then create an instance of ServiceHost.

What are some different ways of implementing WCF Security?

Transport level security, Message security, identity and role based security.

How can one implement SSL security on WCF?

Utilizing transport level security via a web.config configuration or proper setup in an IIS hosted service.

What are the system provided bindings in WCF?

- BasicHttpBinding
- WSHttpBinding
- WSDualHttpBinding
- WSFederationHttpBinding
- NetHttpBinding
- NetHttpsBinding
- NetTcpBinding
- NetNamedPipeBinding
- NetMsmqBinding
- NetPeerTcpBinding
- MsmqIntegrationBinding
- BasicHttpContextBinding
- NetTcpContextBinding

• WebHttpBinding

WSHttpContextBinding

UdpBinding

What are the different WCF instancing modes?

Per Call, Per Session and Single instance mode.

What are the 3 WCF concurrency types?

1. Single: A single request has access to the WCF service object at a given moment of time. So only one request will be processed at any given moment of time. The other requests have to wait until the request processed by the WCF service is completed.

2. Multiple: In this scenario, multiple requests can be handled by the WCF service object at any given moment of time. In other words, requests are processed at the same time by spawning multiple threads on the WCF server object. So you have great throughput here but you need to ensure concurrency issues related to WCF server objects.

3. Reentrant: A single request thread has access to the WCF service object, but the thread can exit the WCF service to call another WCF service or can also call a WCF client through callback and reenter without deadlock.

What is throttling behavior in a WCF service?

WCF throttling helps you to put an upper limit on the number of concurrent calls, WCF instances, and concurrent sessions. WCF provides three ways by which you can define upper limits:

MaxConcurrentCalls,   MaxConcurrentInstances,   and
MaxConcurrentSessions.

CHAPTER 11: SILVERLIGHT QUESTIONS AND ANSWERS

What is Microsoft Silverlight?

• Silverlight is a web based technology, launched by Microsoft in April 2007. Silverlight is considered as a competitor to Adobe's Flash.

• Silverlight is Microsoft's implementation of a cross-browser, cross-platform client framework that allows designers and developers to deliver Rich Internet Applications (RIA) embedded in Web pages.

• Silverlight is a browser plug-in approximately 6MB in size; it is client-side free software, with an easy and fast (less than 10 sec) one time installation available for any client side browser.

• It supports advanced data integration, multithreading, HD video using IIS Smooth Streaming, and built-in content protection. Silverlight enables online and offline applications for a broad range of business and consumer scenarios.

• One of the design goals of the Silverlight technology is to fill the gap between Windows applications and Web applications in terms of creating Graphical User Interfaces (GUI).

• Silverlight applications are run as client-side applications without the need to refresh the browser to update the UI. However, because of the built-in .NET framework, Silverlight applications can easily integrate with server-side controls and services. Using Silverlight's implementation of the .NET framework, developers can easily integrate existing libraries and code into Silverlight applications.

Why architect an application in Silverlight?

• Support for the .NET Framework – if you are already a .NET developer, it is easy to start programming on Silverlight.

• Support for managed code – you can write programs in your favorite language which .NET CLR supports like C#, VB.NET, dynamic languages (IronPython, IronRuby).

• Better development tools -Visual Studio 2010, Expression Blend.

• Large community- More learning resources available compared to Flash.

• Integration with Enterprise based technologies like WPF, LINQ etc...

• Silverlight integrates the XAML declarative language with the .NET framework.

• It is a cross-browser, cross-platform technology which provides a consistent user experience everywhere it runs.

• The Silverlight plug-in installs in seconds, and leaves a very small footprint.

• After you install the plug-in, users no longer need to install anything on their workstations to run Silverlight applications. The applications are available to them from whatever browser they are accessing.

• It runs a client-side application that can read data and update the UI without interrupting the user by refreshing the whole page.

• It can run asynchronous communications with the server, allowing the UI to continue to function while waiting for the server response.

• It delivers rich video, audio, and graphics.

Is Silverlight free?

Yes, Microsoft has made the Silverlight browser plug-in freely available for all supported platforms and browsers.

What is Silverlight Runtime?

Silverlight Runtime is a browser plug-in to support Silverlight enabled applications.

What is a .xap file?

A .xap file is a Silverlight-based application package (.xap) that is generated when the Silverlight project is built. A .xap file is the compressed output file for a Silverlight application. The .xap file includes AppManifest.xaml, the compiled output assembly of the Silverlight project (.dll), and the resource files referred to by the Silverlight application.

What is a Silverlight.js file?

Silverlight.js is a helper file which enables websites to create advanced Silverlight installation and instantiation experiences. You can call the createObject and createObjectEx functions defined in this file to embed the Silverlight plug-in in a web page.

What is the use of the ClientBin folder?

The ClientBin folder is used to place the .xap file of a Silverlight application. You can keep it anywhere in your web application, but this is the default location used by Silverlight.

How would you change the default page of a Silverlight application?

To change the default page of a Silverlight application, you need to set the RootVisual property inside the Application_Startup event of the App.xaml file.

What is XAML?

XAML stands for eXtended Application Markup Language. XAML contains XML that is used to declaratively specify the user interface for Silverlight or WPF applications.

What is the AppManifest.xml file?

The AppManifest.xml file defines the assemblies that get deployed in the client application. This file is automatically updated when compiling your application (including the Runtime version information). Based on the settings of a referenced assembly it is added to the Application manifest.

What files are contained within the .xap file?

The .xap file contains an application manifest (AppManifest.xaml) file and all the necessary DLLs that are required by the application. The first DLL contained is the compiled version of your application and has the same name of your application. In my test, I created an application named "SilverlightApplication1", so the DLL is named "SilverlightApplication1.dll". The rest of the DLLs are the dependencies the application requires.

Can I consume WCF and ASP.NET Web Services in Silverlight?

Yes, you can.

What is the difference between WPF and Silverlight?

Silverlight and Windows Presentation Foundation (WPF) are two different products from Microsoft, but have lot of overlap. Silverlight is a subset of WPF in terms of features and functionality.

Silverlight is a Microsoft technology, competing with Adobe's Flash, and is meant for developing rich browser based internet applications.

WPF is a Microsoft technology meant for developing enhanced graphics applications for the desktop platform. In addition, WPF applications can be hosted on web browsers which offer rich graphics features for web applications. Web Browser Applications (WBA) developed on the WPF technology uses XAML to host user interfaces for browser applications. XAML stands for eXtended Application Markup Language, which is a new declarative programming model from Microsoft. XAML files are hosted as discrete files in the Web server, but are downloaded to the browsers and converted to a user interface by the .NET runtime in the client browsers.

WPF runs on the .NET runtime, and developers can take advantage of the rich .NET Framework and WPF libraries to build really cool Windows applications. WPF supports 3-D graphics, complex animations, hardware acceleration etc.

Silverlight uses a particular implementation of a XAML parser, with that parser being part of the Silverlight core installation. In some cases, the parsing behavior differs from the parsing behavior in Windows Presentation Foundation (WPF), which also has a particular implementation.

What are the different layout controls available in Silverlight?

There are three different types of layout controls provided by Silverlight:

1. Canvas - Position child elements absolutely in x, y space.

2. StackPanel - Position child elements relative to one another in horizontal or vertical stacks.

3. Grid - Position child elements in rows and columns.

Do I need to have the .NET Framework installed in order to use Silverlight?

The answer to this is no - a cross platform version of the .NET Framework is included in the 6 MB Silverlight 4 download, which means you do not need to have anything extra installed on the client in order to access Silverlight applications in the browser.

What is meant by RIA?

RIA stands for Rich Internet Applications, which are Web applications with rich user interfaces including media elements such as audio, video etc. You can think of them as being similar to powerful and rich desktop applications, except that RIA applications are Web based.

What are the design files and the code-behind files in Silverlight?

The user interface elements of Silverlight applications are defined in XAML files. The logic and functionality of Silverlight applications is implemented using managed NET code-behind files that share the same class with the XAML file.

What are .NET RIA Services?

Microsoft .NET RIA Services helps to simplify the n-tier application pattern by combining the ASP.NET and Silverlight platforms. RIA Services provides a pattern using which you can write application logic that can run on the mid-tier and controls access to data for queries, changes, and custom operations. It also provides support for data validation, authentication, and roles by integrating with Silverlight components on the client and ASP.NET on the middle tier.

ENDING NOTES

At this point you should be a programming god (at least as far as an interviewer is concerned).

Remember, you shouldn't just memorize the answer without a thorough understanding of the concepts that lie behind the question and the answer. The best programmers are not always the smartest ones. The best programmers are the ones who spend the countless hours and days understanding not only the language they program in but the concepts that the language conveys. The language just allows the programmer to implement abstractions and it is those abstractions that must be fully understand in order to implement the best applications.

www.ingramcontent.com/pod-product-compliance
Lightning Source LLC
Chambersburg PA
CBHW071206050326
40689CB00011B/2263